Army Department United States, John Pope

The Campaign in Virginia, of July and August 1862

Official Report of Major General John Pope

Army Department United States, John Pope

The Campaign in Virginia, of July and August 1862
Official Report of Major General John Pope

ISBN/EAN: 9783744670555

Printed in Europe, USA, Canada, Australia, Japan

Cover: Foto ©ninafisch / pixelio.de

More available books at **www.hansebooks.com**

CAMPAIGN IN

OF

LY AND A

MILWAUKEE:
JERMAIN & BRIGHTMAN, BOOK AND JOB PRINTERS, BUILDING.
1863.

CAMPAIGN IN VIRGINIA.

GENERAL POPE'S OFFICIAL REPORT.

New York, January 27th, 1863.

GENERAL:

I have the honor to submit the following report of the operations of the army under my command during the late campaign in Virginia :

Several of the reports of Corps Commanders have not yet reached me, but so much time has elapsed since the termination of the campaign, that I do not feel at liberty to withhold this report longer.

The strange misapprehension of facts concerning this campaign, which, though proceeding from irresponsible sources, has much possessed the public mind, makes it necessary for me to enter more into detail than I should otherwise have done, and to embody in the report such of the dispatches and orders sent and received as will make clear every statement which is contained in it.

On the 26th day of June, 1862, by special order of the President of the United States, I was assigned to the command of the Army of Virginia. That army was constituted as follows :

First Corps, under Major-Gen. Fremont.

Second Corps, under Major-Gen. Banks.

Third Corps, under Major-Gen. McDowell.

In addition to these three Corps, a small unorganized force under Brig.-General Sturgis was posted in the neighborhood of Alexandria, and was then in process of being organised for field service. The forces in the entrenchments around Washington were also placed under my command. All the disposable moveable forces consisted of the three Corps first named. Their effective strength of infantry and artillery as reported to me was as follows :

Fremont's Corps, eleven thousand five hundred strong; Banks' Corps, reported at fourteen thousand and five hundred, but in reality only about eight thousand; McDowell's Corps, eighteen thousand four hundred—making a total of thirty-eight thousand men.

The cavalry numbered about five thousand, but most of it was badly mounted and armed, and in poor condition for service. These forces were scattered over a wide district of country, not within supporting distance of each other, and many of the brigades and divisions were badly organized, and in a demoralized condition. This was particularly the case with the Army Corps of Major-Gen. Fremont, a sad report of which was made to me by Gen. Sigel, when he relieved Gen. Fremont in command of the Corps.

My first labors were directed to the reorganization of some of the divisions and brigades of that Corps, and to supplying the whole force with much of the material absolutely necessary for troops in the field.

The Corps of Banks and Fremont were in the Valley of the Shenandoah, between Winchester and Middletown, the bulk of the forces being in the vicinity of the latter place.

One division of McDowell's Corps was at Manassas Junction, with its advance thrown forward to Catlett's Station. The other division was posted in the vicinity of Falmouth, opposite Fredericksburgh.

When I first assumed command of these forces, the troops under Jackson had retired from the Valley of the Shenandoah and were in rapid march toward Richmond, so that, at that time, there was no force of the enemy of any consequence within a week's march of any of the troops assigned to my command.

It was the wish of the Government that I should cover the city of Washington from any attacks from the direction of Richmond, make such dispositions as were necessary to assure the safety of the Valley of the Shenandoah, and at the same time so to operate upon the enemy's lines of communication in the direction of Gordonsville and Charlottsville, as to draw off, if possible, a considerable force of the enemy from Richmond, and thus relieve the operations against that city of the army of the Potomac.

The first object I had in view was to concentrate, as far as possible, all the moveable forces under my command, and to establish them in such positions as best to effect the objects set forth. It seemed to me that the security of the Shenandoah Valley was not best attained by posting troops within the Valley itself, but that the necessary results could be better accomplished, and the other objects with which I was charged best promoted, by concentrating these forces at some point or points from which, if any attempts were made to enter the Valley of the Shenandoah from Richmond, I should be able, by rapid marching, to interpose between such force and the main body of the enemy, and cut off its retreat. I felt confident, and this confidence was justified by subsequent results, that no considerable force of the enemy would attempt to enter the Valley of the Shenandoah while the forces under my command were so posted as to be able without difficulty to intercept its retreat and fall upon its rear.— I accordingly sent orders to Maj.-Gen. Sigel, commanding the First Corps, to move forward from Middletown, cross the Shenandoah at Front Royal, and pursuing the west side of the Blue Ridge, to take post at Sperryville, by passing through Luray Gap. At the same time I directed Major-Gen. Banks, crossing the Shenandoah at the same point, to move forward and take post between six and ten miles east of Sperryville. Gen. McDowell was ordered to move Ricketts' Division of his Corps from Manassas Junction to Waterloo Bridge, the point where the turnpike from Warrenton to Sperryville crosses the Upper Rappahannock. King's Division of the same Corps it was thought best to leave at Fredericksburgh, to cover the crossing of the Rappahannock at that point, and to protect the railroad thence to Aquia Creek, and the public buildings which had been erected at the latter place. While I yielded to this wish of the War Department, the wide separation of this division from the main body of the army, and the ease with which the enemy would be able to interpose between them engaged my earnest attention and gave me very serious uneasiness.

While these movements were in progress, commenced the series of battles which preceded and attended the retreat of Gen. McClellan from the Chickahominy toward Harrison's landing. When first Gen. McClellan began to intimate by his dispatches that he designed making this movement towards James River, I suggested to the President of the United States the impolicy of such a movement, and the serious consequences which would be likely to result from it, and urged upon him that he should send orders to Gen. McClellan that if he were unable to maintain his position upon the Chickahominy, and were pressed by superior forces of the enemy, to mass his whole force on the north side of that stream, even at the risk of losing much material of war, and endeavor to make his way in the direction of Hanover Court House; but in no event to retreat with his army further to the South than the White House on York River. I stated to the President that the retreat to James River was carrying Gen McClellan away from any reinforcements that could possibly be sent him within a reasonable time, and was absolutely depriving him of any substantial aid from the forces under my command; that by this movement the whole army of the enemy would be interposed between his army and mine, and that they would then be at liberty to strike in either direction, as they might consider it most advantageous; that this movement to James River would leave entirely unprotected, except in so far as the small force under my command was able to protect it, the whole region in front of Washington, and that it would then, therefore, be impossible to send any of the forces under my command to reinforce Gen. McClellan without rendering it certain that the enemy, even in the worst case for themselves, would have the privilege and power of exchanging Richmond for Washington City; that to them the loss of Richmond would be trifling, while the loss of Washington to us would be conclusive, or nearly so, in its results upon this war. I was so deeply impressed with these views that I repeatedly and earnestly urged them upon the President and the Secretary of War.

After Gen. McClellan had taken up his position at Harrison's Landing, I addressed to him a letter, stating my position and the distribution of the troops under my command, and requesting him, in all earnestness and good faith, to write me fully and freely his views, and to suggest to me any measures which he thought desirable to enable me to co-operate with him, or to render any assistance in my power in the operations of the army under his command. I stated to him that I had no object except to assist his operations, and that I would undertake any labor and run any risk for that purpose. I therefore desired him to feel no hesitation in communicating freely with me, as he might rest assured that every suggestion that he would make would meet all respect and consideration at my hands, and that so far as it was in my power to do so, I would carry out his wishes with all energy, and with all the means at my command. In reply to this communication, I received a letter from Gen. McClellan, very general in terms, and proposing nothing toward the accomplishment of the purpose I had suggested to him. It became apparent that, considering the situation in which the Army of the Potomac and the Army of Virginia were placed in relation to each other, and the absolute necessity of harmonious and prompt co-operation between them, some military superior both of Gen. McClellan and myself should be called to Washington and placed in command of all the operations in Virginia. In accordance with these views, Major-Gen. Halleck was called to Washington and placed in general command. Many circumstances, which it is not necessary here to set forth, induced me to express to the President, to the Secretary of War, and to Gen. Halleck, my desire to be relieved from the command of the Army of Virginia, and to be returned to the Western country. My services, however, were considered necessary in the projected campaign, and my wishes were not complied with. I accordingly took the field in Virginia with grave forebodings of the result, but with a determination to carry out the plans of the Government with all the energy and with all the ability of which I was master.

Previous to taking the field I issued the following orders,* which set out very fully the policy which I considered advisable, and which, at the time, received the sanction of the Government, and, so far as I know, the approval of the country.

The order requiring the troops to subsist upon the country in which their operations were conducted has, with a wilful disregard of its terms, been construed greatly to my discredit, as authorizing indiscriminate robbery and plunder. Yet the terms of this order are so specific as to the manner and by whom all property or subsistence needed for the use of the army should be seized, and the order is so common in the history of warfare, that I have been amazed that it could be so misinterpreted and misunderstood. It is, therefore, submitted here for the calm examination of the Government and of the public. I believed then, and believe now, that the policy there laid down was wise and just, and was well calculated to secure efficient and rapid operations of the army; and in case of reverse, to leave the enemy without the means of subsisting in the country over which our army had passed, and over which any pursuit must be conducted. The long delay and embarrassment of the army under General Lee, in its subsequent movements toward Washington, occasioned largely by the want of supplies taken from the country under this order, fully justified its wisdom.

*See Appendix.

It was determined, before I left Washington to take the field in Virginia, that the union of the armies of Virginia and of the Potomac was absolutely essential both to the safety of the National Capital and to the further successful prosecution of the operations against Richmond. The mission of the army under my command, therefore, was to cover as far as possible the front of Washington, and make secure the Valley of the Shenandoah, and so to operate upon the enemy's lines of communication to the west and northwest, as to force him to make such heavy detachments from his main force at Richmond as would enable the Army of the Potomac to withdraw from its position at Harrison's Landing; and to take shipping for Aquia Creek or for Alexandria; and if, as was feared, the enemy should throw his whole force in the direction of Washington, it became my duty to resist his advance at all hazards, and so to delay and embarrass his movement as to gain all the time possible for the arrival of the Army of the Potomac behind the Rappahannock.

Meantime, before the arrival of Gen. Halleck, I instructed Gen. King, at Fredericksburg, to send forward detachments of his cavalry to operate upon the line of the Virginia Central Railroad, and as far as possible to embarrass and destroy communication between Richmond and the Valley of the Shenandoah. Several cavalry expeditions which that officer dispatched for the purpose were completely successful, and succeeded in breaking up the railroad at several points upon several occasions. At the same time I directed Maj.-Gen. Banks to send forward an infantry brigade, with all his cavalry, to march rapidly upon Culpepper Court House, and after taking possession of that place, to push forward cavalry toward the Rapidan, in the direction of Gordonsville. On the 14th of July, after this movement was successfully accomplished, I directed Gen. Banks to push forward during the night of that day, the whole of his cavalry force under Brig.-Gen. Hatch from Culpepper, with orders to take possession of Gordonsville, and to destroy the railroad for ten or fifteen miles east of that place, with a portion of this force, whilst the remainder should be pushed forward in the direction of Charlottesville, to destroy the railroad bridges and interrupt that line of communications as far as practicable.

At that time there was no force of the enemy at Gordonsville or in the vicinity, and the whole operation as ordered was not only easily practicable, but would have been attended with serious consequences to the enemy; but to my surprise and dissatisfaction, I received, on the 17th of July, from Gen. Banks, a report that Gen. Hatch had taken with him infantry, artillery and trains of wagons, and that in consequences of bad roads he had at that date only succeeded in going as far as Madison Court House. Meantime, on the 16th of July, the advance of Jackson's forces, under Ewell, had reached Gordonsville, and the proposed movement, as ordered, became impracticable. No satisfactory explanation has ever been made to me of the departure from my orders on the part of Gen. Hatch. Finding it no longer practicable to occupy Gordonsville as I had designed, I sent orders to Gen. Banks to direct Gen. Hatch to select from his own cavalry and that of Gen. McDowell, which I had sent forward, fifteen hundred to two thousand of the best mounted men, and to proceed from Madison Court House around the west side of the Blue Ridge, to a point whence he could make an easy descent upon the railroad west of Gordonsville, and, if successful, to push forward to Charlottesville, and if possible destroy the railroad between that place and Lynchburg. In compliance with this order, Gen. Hatch commenced to make the movement as directed, but abandoned it very soon after he started, and returned by the way of Sperryville to his post. As soon as I had received the report of this second failure, I relieved Gen. Hatch from the command of the cavalry of Gen. Banks' corps, and sent Brig.-Gen. Buford to report to Gen. Banks as the Chief of Cavalry of his corps.

On the 29th of July I left Washington, and, after reviewing Ricketts' division of McDowell's Corps at Waterloo Bridge, repaired to the headquarters of Gen. Banks, a few miles southeast of Little Washington. All preparations having been completed, I instructed Gen. Banks to move forward on the 7th of August, and take post at the point where the turnpike from Sperryville to Culpepper crosses the Hazel River. Gen. McDowell was ordered on the day previous to move forward with Ricketts' division from Waterloo Bridge to Culpepper Court House, so that on the 7th of August all the infantry and artillery forces of the Army of Virginia were assembled along the turnpike from Sperryville to Culpepper, and numbered about 28,000 men. Gen. King's division, as I have before stated, was left on the Lower Rappahannock, opposite Fredericksburg, and was not then available for active operations in the direction of Gordonsville. The cavalry forces covering the front of the army on that day, were distributed as follows : Gen. Buford, with five regiments, was posted at Madison Court House, with his pickets along the line of the Rapidan, from Burnett's Ford as far west as the Blue Ridge. Gen. Sigel had been directed to post a brigade of infantry and a battery of artillery at the point where the road from Madison Court House to Sperryville crosses Robertson's River, as a support to the cavalry of Gen. Buford, in front of him. Gen. Bayard, with four regiments of cavalry, was posted near Rapidan Station, the point where the Orange and Alexandria road crosses Rapidan River, with his pickets extended as far to the east as Raccoon Ford, and connecting with Gen. Buford on his right at Burnett's Ford. From Raccoon Ford to the forks of the Rappahannock, above Falmouth, the Rapidan was lined with cavalry pickets. On the top of Thoroughfare Mountain, about half-way between Gens. Bayard and Buford, was established a signal station, which overlooked the whole country as far south as Orange Court House.

On the 7th I proceeded to Sperryville, and inspected the Corps of Major-Gen. Sigel. I remained at Sperryville until 4 o'clock in the afternoon of that day, during which time I received several reports from the front that the enemy was crossing the Rappahannock at several points between the railroad crossing of that river and Liberty

Mills. I reached Culpepper Court House on the morning of the 8th of August. The town had been occupied for several days by Crawford's Brigade of Gen. Banks' Corps; and on the 7th Ricketts' Division of McDowell's Corps had also reached there from Waterloo Bridge. During the whole of the morning of the 8th, I continued to receive reports from Gen. Bayard, who was slowly falling back in the direction of Culpepper Court House, from the advance of the enemy; and from Gen. Buford, who also reported the enemy advancing in heavy force upon Madison Court House. My instructions required me to be careful and keep my communications good with Fredericksburgh, and by no means to permit the enemy to interpose between me and that place. Although during the whole of the 8th of August, it was very doubtful, from the reports of Gens. Bayard and Buford, whether the enemy's movement was in the direction of Madison Court House or of Culpepper, I considered it advisable, in view of my relations with Fredericksburgh, to concentrate my whole force in the direction of Culpepper, so as to keep myself constantly interposed between the main body of the enemy and the lower fords of the Rappahannock. Early in the day I pushed forward Crawford's Brigade of Banks' Corps, in the direction of Cedar or Slaughter Mountain, to support Gen. Bayard, who was falling back in the direction, and to assist him as far as practicable in determining the movements and the forces of the enemy. I sent orders also to Gen. Banks to move forward promptly from Hazel River to Culpepper Court House, and also to Gen. Sigel to march at once from Sperryville to the same place. To my surprise, I received, after night on the 8th, a note from Gen. Sigel, dated at Sperryville, at 6 1-2 o'clock that afternoon, asking me by what road he should march to Culpepper Court House. As there was but one road between those two points, and that a broad stone turnpike, I was at a loss to understand how Gen. Sigel could entertain any doubt as to the road by which he should march. This doubt, however, delayed the arrival of his Corps at Culpepper Court House several hours, and rendered it impracticable for that Corps to be pushed to the front, as I had designed, on the afternoon of the next day.

Early on the morning of the 9th of August, I directed Gen. Banks to move forward toward Cedar Mountain with his whole Corps, and to join the brigade of that Corps, under Gen. Crawford, which had been pushed forward on the day previous. I directed Gen. Banks to take up a strong position at or near the point occupied by that brigade, to check the advance of the enemy, and to determine his forces and the character of his movements as far as practicable. The consolidated report of Gen. Banks' Corps, received some days previously, exhibited an effective force of something over 14,000 men. Appended to this report will be found the return in question. It appeared subsequently however, that Gen. Banks' forces at that time did not exceed 8,000 men. But although I several times called Gen. Banks' attention to the discrepancy between this return and the force he afterward stated to me he had led to the front, that discrepancy has never been explained, and I do not yet understand how Gen. Banks could have been so greatly mistaken as to the forces under his immmediate command.

I directed him when he went forward from Culpepper Court House, if the enemy advanced to attack him in the strong position which I had instructed him to take up, that he should push his skirmishers well to the front and notify me immediately. Three miles in his rear and within easy supporting distance, Ricketts' Division of McDowell's Corps had been posted at the point where the road from Madison Court House to Culpepper intersects the road from Culpepper to Cedar Mountain. This division was so posted because it was not certain whether a considerable force of the enemy was not advancing on Culpepper from the direction of Madison Court House, Gen. Buford having reported to me very early on the morning of the 9th from Madison Court House that the enemy was in heavy force on his right, his left, and partly on his rear, and that he was retreating in the direction of Sperryville.

Desultory artillery firing had been kept up all day on the 9th, in the direction of Gen. Banks' Corps, but I continued to receive, during the whole of that day, reports from Gen. Banks that no considerable force of the enemy had come forward, that his cavalry had been ostentatiously displayed, but that he did not believe that the enemy was in sufficient force to make any attack upon him. As late as 5 o'clock in the afternoon, Gen. Banks wrote me substantially to the same effect; but before I had received this last note, the artillery firing had become so rapid and continuous, that I feared a general engagement was going on, or might be brought on at any moment. I therefore instructed Gen. McDowell to move forward Ricketts' Division rapidly to the field, and accompanied that division myself. At no time during the day did Gen. Banks express any apprehensions of attack in force by the enemy, nor did he ask, nor intimate that he needed reinforcements.

Gen. Sigel's Corps began to march into Culpepper Court House late in the afternoon, and just as I was leaving that place, having been delayed several hours by Gen. Sigel's singular uncertainty as to what road he ought to pursue. I had given orders a number of days previously that all the troops belonging to the Army of Virginia should be ready to march at the shortest notice, and should habitually keep two day's cooked rations in their haversacks. Notwithstanding this order, Gen. Sigel's Corps arrived in Culpepper without any rations, and was unable to move forward until provisions could be procured from McDowell's train, and cooked at Culpepper Court House.

I have received no report from Gen. Banks of his operations at Cedar Mountain, but I had sent forward Brig.-Gen. Roberts, Chief of Cavalry, of my Staff, and had directed him to report to Gen. Banks in the early part of the day of the 9th, and to advise freely with him as to the operations of his Corps. Gen. Roberts, as well as Gen. Banks, was fully advised of my wishes, and that I desired Gen. Banks merely to keep the enemy in check, by occupying a strong position in his front, until the whole of the disposable force under my command should be concentrated in the neighborhood. Gen. Roberts reported to me that he had conferred freely with Gen. Banks, and urgently represented to him my purposes, but that Gen. Banks, contrary to his suggestions and my wishes, had left the strong position which he had taken up, and had advanced two miles to assault the enemy, believing that they were not in considerable force, and that he would be able to crush their advance before their main body could come up from the direction of the Rapidan. He accordingly threw forward his whole Corps into action, against superior forces of the enemy, strongly posted and sheltered by woods and ridges. His advance led him over the open ground, which was everywhere swept by the fire of the enemy, concealed in woods and ravines beyond. Notwithstanding these disadvantages, his Corps gallantly responded to his orders, and assaulted the enemy with great fury and determination. The action lasted about an hour and a half, and during that time our forces suffered heavy loss, and were gradually driven back to their former position, at which point, just at dusk, Ricketts' Division of McDowell's Corps came up and joined in the engagement.

As soon as I arrived on the field, at the head of Ricketts' Division, I directed Gen. Banks to draw in his right, which was much extended, and to mass the whole of his right wing at the centre of his line, pushing forward at the same time Ricketts' Division to occupy the ground thus vacated. The enemy followed Banks as he retired with great caution, and emerging from the woods which had sheltered him all day, attempted to push forward to the open ground in front of our new line. A sharp artillery engagement immediately commenced, when the enemy was driven back to the woods, principally by the batteries of Ricketts' Division. The artillery firing was kept up until near midnight of the 9th. Finding that Banks' Corps had been severely cut up, and was much fatigued, I drew it back to the rear, and pushed forward the Corps of Sigel, which had began to arrive, to occupy the woods on the left of the road, with a wide space of open ground in his front. Ricketts' Division was also drawn back to the cover of the woods and behind the ridges in the open ground on the right of Sigel. These dispositions were completed about daybreak on the morning of the 10th. Banks' Corps, reduced to about 5,000 men, was so cut up, and worn down with fatigue, that I did not consider it capable of rendering any efficient service for several days. I therefore directed Gen. Banks, or in his absence Gen. Williams, who succeeded to the command, to assemble his Corps on the road to Culpepper Court House, and about two miles in rear of our front, to collect his stragglers, send back his wounded to Culpepper Court House, and proceed as rapidly as possible to put the Corps in condition for service. In consequence of the vigorous resistance of the night previous, and the severe loss of the enemy in trying to advance, before daylight of the 10th, Jackson drew back his forces toward Cedar Mountain, about two miles from our front. Our pickets were immediately pushed forward, supported by Milroy's Brigade, and occupied the ground.

The day of the 10th was intensely hot, and the troops on both sides were too much fatigued to renew the action. My whole effective force on that day, exclusive of Banks' Corps, which was in no condition for service, was about 20,000 artillery and infantry, and about 2,000 cavalry—Gen. Buford, with the cavalry force under his command, not yet having been able to join the main body. I had telegraphed Gen. King at Fredericksburg to move forward on the 8th, by the lower fords of the Rappahannock and Stevensburg, to join me. A large part of his command had just returned from a very fatiguing expedition against the Central Railroad, but he marched forward promptly and joined the main body late in the evening of the 11th. The whole day was spent by both armies in burying the dead and in bringing off the wounded.

Although, even after King joined me, my whole effective force was barely equal to that of the enemy, I determined, after giving King's Division one night's rest, to fall upon him at daylight on the 12th on his line of communications, and compel him to fight a battle, which must have been entirely decisive for one army or the other. But during the night of the 11th, Jackson evacuated the positions in front of us, and retreated rapidly across the Rapidan, in the direction of Gordonsville, leaving many of his dead and wounded on the field and along the road from Cedar Mountain to Orange Court House. No material of war nor baggage trains were lost on either side, but the loss of life on both sides was severe. Brig.-Gens. Geary, Auger and Carrol were badly wounded, and Brig.-Gen. Prince was captured by accident. Very many of our best field and company officers were killed or wounded. From the verbal reports and statements of Gen. Banks and others, the Massachusetts regiments behaved with especial gallantry, and sustained the heaviest losses, but the conduct of the whole Corps of Gen. Banks was beyond all praise.

Although I regret that Gen. Banks thought it expedient to depart from my instructions, it gives me pleasure to bear testimony to his gallant and intrepid conduct throughout the action. He exposed himself as freely as any one under his command, and his example went far to secure that gallant and noble conduct which has made his Corps famous. Generals Williams, Geary, Auger, Carroll, Gordon, Crawford and Green behaved with distinguished gallantry. Gen. Prince, who led his brigade throughout the action with coolness and courage, was captured after dark while passing from one portion of his command to the other. As I have not received any report from Gen. Banks, it is not in my power to mention the field and company officers who distinguished themselves under his immediate eye in action; but as soon as his report is received, I will transmit it to the Government, and endeavor to do justice to every officer and soldier who belonged to his Corps. Brig.-Gen. Roberts, Chief of Cavalry, of my Staff, accompanied Gen. Banks throughout the day, and rendered most important and gallant service.

No report of killed and wounded has been made to me by Gen. Banks. I can, therefore, only form an approximation of our losses in that battle. Our killed, wounded and prisoners amounted to about 1,800 men, besides which fully 1,000 men straggled back to Culpepper Court House and beyond, and never entirely returned to their commands.

A strong cavalry force, under Gens. Buford and Bayard, pursued the enemy to the Rapidan, and captured many stragglers. The cavalry forces immediately resumed their original position, and again occupied the Rapidan from Raccoon Ford to the base of the Blue Ridge. On the 14th of August, Gen. Reno, with 8,000 men of the forces which had arrived at Falmouth under Gen. Burnside, joined me. I immediately pushed forward my whole force in the direction of the Rapidan, and occupied a strong position, with my right, under Maj.-Gen. Sigel, resting on Robertson's River, where the road from Cedar mountain to Orange Court House crosses that stream; my center, under Gen. McDowell, occupied both flanks of Cedar Mountain; and my left, under Gen. Reno, a position near Raccoon Ford, and covering the road from that ford to Stevensburg and Culpepper. I began again, immediately, to operate with my cavalry upon the enemy's communications with Richmond. From the 12th to the 18th of August, reports were constantly reaching me of large forces of the enemy reinforcing Jackson from the direction of Richmond, and by the morning of the 18th, I became satisfied that nearly the whole force of the enemy from Richmond was assembling in my front, along the south side of the Rapidan, and extending from Raccoon Ford to Liberty Mills. The cavalry expedition sent out on the 16th, in the direction of Louisa Court House, captured the Adjutant-General of General Stuart, and was very near capturing that officer himself. Among the papers taken was an autograph letter of Gen. Robert Lee to Gen. Stuart, dated Gordonsville, Aug. 15, which made manifest to me the position and force of the enemy, and their determination to overwhelm the army under my command before it could be reinforced by any portion of the Army of the Potomac. I held on to my position thus far to the front, for the purpose of affording all the time possible for the arrival of the Army of the Potomac at Aquia and Alexandria, and to embarrass and delay the movements of the enemy as far as practicable.

On the 18th of August it became apparent to me that this advanced position, with the small force under my command, was no longer tenable in the face of the overwhelming forces of the enemy. I determined, accordingly, to withdraw behind the Rappahannock with all speed, and, as I had been instructed, to defend, as far as practicable, the line of that river. I accordingly directed Maj.-Gen. Reno to send back his trains on the morning of the 18th, by the way of Stevensburg to Kelly's or Barnett's Ford, and as soon as the trains had gotten several hours in advance, to follow them with his whole Corps, and take post behind the Rappahannock, leaving all his cavalry in the neighborhood of Raccoon Ford to cover this movement. Gen. Banks' Corps, which had been ordered on the 12th to take position at Culpepper Court House, I directed, with its trains preceding it, to cross the Rappahannock at the point where the Orange and Alexandria Railroad crosses that river; Gen. McDowell's train was ordered to pursue the same route; while the train of Gen. Sigel was directed through Jefferson to cross the Rappahannock at Warrenton, Sulphur

Springs. So soon as these trains had been sufficiently advanced, Mc-Dowell's Corps was directed to take the route from Culpepper to Rappahannock Ford, while Gen. Sigel, who was on the right and front, was directed to follow the movement of his train to Sulphur Springs. These movements were executed during the day and night of the 18th, and the day of the 19th, by which time the whole army with its trains had safely recrossed the Rappahannock and was posted behind that stream, with its left at Kelly's Ford, and its right about three miles above Rappahannock Station, Gen Sigel having been directed immediately upon crossing at Sulphur Springs to march down the left bank of the Rappahannock, until he connected closely with Gen. McDowell's right.

Early in the morning of the 20th, the enemy drove in our pickets in front of Kelly's Ford, and at Rappahannock Station; but, finding we had covered these fords, and that it would be impracticable to force the passage of the river without heavy loss, his advance halted, and the main body of his army was brought forward from the Rapidan. By the night of the 20th, the bulk of his forces confronted us from Kelly's Ford to a point above our extreme right. During the whole of the 21st and 22d, efforts were made by the enemy at various points to cross the river, but they were repulsed in all cases. The artillery firing was rapid and continuous during the whole of those days, and extended along the line of the river for seven or eight miles. Finding that it was not practicable to force the passage of the river in my front, the enemy began slowly to move up the river, for the purpose of turning our right. My orders required me to keep myself closely in communication with Fredericksburg, to which point the Army of the Potomac was being brought from the Peninsula, with the purpose of reinforcing me from that place by the line of the Rappahannock. My force was too small to enable me to extend my right further, without so weakening my line as to render it easy for the enemy to break through it at any point. I telegraphed again and again to Washington, representing this movement of the enemy toward my right, and the impossibility of my being able to extend my lines so as to resist it without abandoning my connections with Fredericksburg. I was assured on the 21st, that if I would hold the line of the river two days longer, I should be so strongly reinforced as not only to be secure, but to be able to resume offensive operations; but on the 25th of August, the only forces that had joined me, or were in the neighborhood, were 2,500 men of the Pennsylvania Reserves, under Brig.-Gen. Reynolds, who had arrived at Kelly's Ford, and the Division of Gen. Kearney, 4,500 strong, which had reached Warrenton Junction.

The line of the Rappahannock is very week, and scarce opposes any considerable obstacle to the advance of an army. It is but a small stream above the forks, and can be crossed by good fords every mile or two of its whole length. The movement of the enemy toward my right occasioned me much uneasiness, in consequence of the instructions, which bound me to keep in close communication with Fredericksburg; but I instructed Gen. Sigel, who occupied the right of my line, and who expressed great apprehension that his flank would be turned, and proposed to withdraw from his position toward the railroad, to stand firm and hold his ground, and to allow the enemy to cross at Sulphur Springs and develop himself on the road toward Warrenton; that, as soon as any considerable force had crossed at that place, I would rapidly mass my army during the night and throw it upon any force of the enemy which attempted to march in the direction of Warrenton. The whole of the cavalry under Brig.-Gens. Buford and Bayard was pushed considerably to the right of Gen. Sigel, in the direction of Fayetteville and Sulphur Springs, to watch the movements of the enemy in that direction, and to picket the river as far up as possible. Gen. Sigel was ordered, if any force of the enemy attempted to cross below Sulphur Springs, to march at once against it and to notify me, as I was determined to resist the passage of the river at any point below the Springs. Copies of my dispatches to the General-in-Chief, and of his replies, the dispatches from Gen. Sigel, and my orders to him given during the 20th, 21st, 22d and 23d of August, are appended, which show completely the condition of things, my understanding of the movements of the enemy, and the dispositions which I made and proposed to make in relation to them.

Finding that the continued movement of the enemy to my right, while heavy masses of his force still confronted me at Rappahannock Station, would within a day, if allowed to continue, either render my position on the Rappahannock wholly untenable, or force me to give battle to the enemy in my front and on my right, I determined, on the afternoon of the 22d, to mass my whole force, to recross the Rappahannock by the bridges and fords near Rappahannock Station, and by Kelly's Ford below, and to fall on the flank and rear of the long column of the enemy which was passing up the river toward our right. I accordingly made the necessary orders on the night of the 22d of August. The attempt would have been dangerous, but no recourse was left me except to make this attack, to retire to Warrenton Junction and abandon the line of the Rappahannock, or to retire in the direction of Fredericksburg, and abandon the Orange and Alexandria Railroad, and the direct approaches to Washington City. I determined, therefore, to hazard the result, and to fall furiously with my whole army on the flank and rear of the enemy. During the night of the 22d a heavy rain set in, which, before day dawned on the 23d, had caused the river to rise six or eight feet, carried away all our bridges, and destroyed all the fords on the river. To recross the Rappahannock, and to make the attack as proposed, was no longer practicable; but the rise in the river which had prevented this movement I believed would also prevent the retreat of that portion of the enemy which had crossed at Sulphur Springs and Waterloo Bridge, according to the reports which had been sent me by Gen. Sigel.

Early on the morning of the 23d, therefore, I massed my whole force in the neighborhood of Rappahannock Station, with the purpose of falling upon that portion of the enemy which had crossed above me, and was then supposed to be between Sulphur Springs, Waterloo Bridge and the town of Warrenton. As the river was too high to be crossed, and was likely to remain so for at least thirty-six hours, I had no fear that the enemy would be able to interpose between me and Fredericksburg, or to make any attempt upon the Orange and Alexandria Railroad north of the Rappahannock. I directed Gen. Sigel to march with his whole Corps upon Sulphur Springs, supported by Reno's Corps and Banks' Corps, to fall upon anybody of the enemy that he might encounter, and to push forward along the river to Waterloo Bridge. I directed Gen. McDowell to move at the same time directly upon the town of Warrenton, so that from that point he would be able, if necessary, to unite with Gen. Sigel on the road from that place to Sulphur Springs, or to Waterloo Bridge. To the Corps of Gen. McDowell I had attached the Pennsylvania Reserves, under Brig.-Gen. Reynolds, the first of the Army of the Potomac that had joined my command.

On the night of the 22d of August a small cavalry force of the enemy, crossing Waterloo Bridge and passing through Warrenton, made a raid upon our trains at Catlett's Station, and destroyed four or five wagons in all, belonging to the train of my own headquarters. At the time this cavalry force attacked at Catlett's, and it certainly was not more than three hundred strong, our whole army-trains were parked at that place, and were guarded by not less than fifteen hundred infantry and five companies of cavalry. The success of this small cavalry party of the enemy, although very trifling and attended with but little damage, was most disgraceful to the force which had been left in charge of the trains.

Gen. Sigel moved as ordered, slowly up the Rappahannock, in the direction of Sulphur Springs, on the 23d, and first encountered a force of the enemy near the point where a small creek called "Great Run" puts into the Rappahannock, about two miles below the Sulphur Springs. The enemy was driven across the stream but destroyed the bridges. The heavy rains had caused this small creek to rise so much that it was not then fordable, so that the night of the 23d and part of the morning of the 24th were spent by Gen. Sigel in rebuilding the bridges. On the night of the 23d, also, the advance of McDowell's Corps occupied Warrenton, a cavalry force of the enemy having retreated from there a few hours before.

On the morning of the 24th, Gen. Sigel, supported by Gens. Reno and Banks, crossed Great Run and occupied the Sulphur Springs, under a heavy fire of artillery from batteries which the enemy had established all along the south side of the Rappahannock. The bridge which had been built at Sulphur Springs, and upon which the forces of the enemy which had crossed a day or two previous escaped from the advance of Gen. Sigel was destroyed, and Gen. Sigel pushed forward with the force supporting him, in the direction of Waterloo Bridge.

Meantime, I had dispatched Brig.-Gen. Buford with a heavy cavalry force from Warrenton, on the morning of the 24th, to reconnoitre the country in the vicinity of Waterloo Bridge, and to interrupt the passage of the river at that point as far as possible. It was then believed by Gen. Sigel, who so reported to me, that a considerable force of the enemy was on the north side of the Rappahannock, and was retiring from his advance in the direction of Waterloo Bridge. By noon of the 24th Gen. Buford reported to me that he had occupied Waterloo Bridge, without finding any force of the enemy, and he did not believe that there was any force between that place and Sulphur Springs. I directed him to destroy the bridge at Waterloo, and to maintain his position until the arrival of the advance of Gen. Sigel. I at once informed Gen. Sigel of these facts, and directed him to push forward his advance to Waterloo. Milroy's Brigade, constituting the advance of his Corps, reached Waterloo late in the afternoon of the 24th. On that afternoon the whole force of the enemy was stretched along the line of the river, from the Rappahannock Station to Waterloo Bridge, with his centre, and I think his main body, in the vicinity of Sulphur Springs. During the day of the 24th, a large detachment of the enemy, numbering thirty-six regiments of infantry, with the usual number of batteries of artillery and a considerable cavalry force, marched rapidly to the north in the direction of Rectortown. They could be plainly seen from our signal stations, established at high points along the Rappahannock; and their movements and force were reported to me from time to time by Col. J. S. Clark, of Gen. Banks' staff, who, on that day, and for many preceding and succeeding days, gave me most valuable and reliable information. I am glad to express here my appreciation of the valuable services of this officer.

On the night of the 24th, my forces were distributed as follows: Ricketts' Division, of McDowell's Corps, on the road from Warrenton to Waterloo Bridge, and about four miles east of Waterloo; King's Division, of the same Corps, between Warrenton and the Sulphur Springs; Sigel's Corps, near the Rappahannock, with his advance at Waterloo Bridge, and his rear in the direction of Sulphur Springs. In his rear, and immediately in contact with him, was Banks' Corps; while Reno's Corps was east and very near the Sulphur Springs.

I was satisfied that no force of the enemy was on the north side of the Rappahannock; but I feared that during the next day—by which time the river would have fallen sufficiently to be passable at any of the fords—the enemy would make an attempt to cross at Rappahannock Station, or at the fords between that point and Sulphur Springs. Yet, as we were confronted at Waterloo Bridge and Sulphur Springs by the main body of the enemy, still moving toward our right, and as the heavy column mentioned previously, was marching with all speed in the direction of White Plains and Salem, and from those points would be able to turn our right by the direction of Thoroughfare Gap, or even north of that place, it was with the greatest reluctance, and only because I felt bound to do so under my instructions, that I took measures again to assure my communications with Fredericksburg. I append herewith orders and dispatches sent and received during the 23d and 24th of August, which will of themselves furnish a succinct account of the movements here set forth, and all the information and assurances upon which those movements were made.

On the 23d I received a dispatch from the General-in-Chief, informing me that heavy reinforcements would begin to arrive at Warrenton Junction the succeeding day, and on the 24th I received dispatches from Col. Haupt, the Railroad Superintendent at Alexandria, who informed me that 30,000 men, ordered forward to join me, had demanded transportation from him, and that they would all be shipped that afternoon or early the next morning. The force which I thus expected was, as reported to me, to consist of the Division of Gen. Sturgis, 10,000 strong; the Division of Gen. Cox, 7,000 strong; the Corps of Gen. Heintzelman, 10,000 strong; and the Corps of Gen. Franklin, 10,000 strong. By the night of the 25th it became apparent to me that I could no longer keep open my communications with Fredericksburg, and oppose the crossing of the Rappahannock, at Rappahannock Station, without abandoning the road from Warrenton to Washington, and leaving open to the enemy the route through Thoroughfare Gap, and all other roads north of the Orange and Alexandria Railroad. As the main body of his force was constantly tending in that direction, I determined no longer to attempt to mask the lower fords of the Rappahannock, but to assemble such forces as I had along the Warrenton Turnpike, between Warrenton and Gainesville, and give battle to the enemy on my right or left, as he might choose. I therefore directed McDowell to occupy Warrenton with his own and Sigel's Corps, supporting him by Banks' Corps from the direction of Fayetteville. I pushed Reno forward to occupy a point near the Warrenton turnpike, and about three miles to the east of that town. I sent orders to Gen. Porter, who had reported to me by note from the neighborhood of Bealeton Station, to push forward and join Reno. Heintzelman's Corps, which had reached Warrenton Junction, was ordered to remain for the present at that point, it being my purpose to push forward that Corps, as soon as practicable, to Greenwich, about half way between Warrenton and Gainesville. I sent orders to Col. Haupt to direct one of the strongest Divisions being sent forward to take post in the works at Manassas Junction, and requested Gen. Halleck to push Franklin with all speed to Gainesville; that he could march quite as rapidly as he could be transported by rail, with the limited means of railroad transportation in our possession, and that his baggage and supplies could be sent forward to Gainesville by rail. I also sent orders to the Colonel commanding at Manassas Junction, for the first Division that reached there from Alexandria to halt and take post in the works at that place, and directed him to push forward all of his cavalry in the direction of Thoroughfare Gap, to watch any movements the enemy might make from that direction. I had instructed Gen. Sturges, commanding at Alexandria, on the 22d of August, to post strong guards along the Railroad from Manassas Junction to Catlett's Station, and requested him to superintend this in person. I also directed Gen. Kearney, who reached Warrenton Junction on the 23d, to see that sufficient guards were placed all along the railroad in his rear. After these precautions and assurances, I had thought and confidently expected that by the afternoon of the 26th, Franklin would have been at or near Gainesville; one Division would have been occupying the works at Manassas Junction; and that the forces under Sturgis and Cox would have been at Warrenton Junction, whence they could at once have been pushed north in the direction of Warrenton Turnpike The orders for the disposition of the forces under my command were sent, and the movements made, so far as practicable, during the day of the 26th.

About 8 o'clock at night on the 26th, the advance of Jackson's force having passed through Thoroughfare Gap, cut the railroad in the neighborhood of Kettle Run, about six miles east of Warrenton Junction. The cavalry force which I had sent forward to Thoroughfare Gap on the morning of the 26th made no report to me. The moment our communications were interrupted at Kettle Run, I was satisfied that the troops which had been promised me from the direction of Washington, had made no considerable progress. Had Franklin been even at Centreville on the 26th, or had Cox and Sturgis been as far west as Bull Run on that day, the movement of Jackson through Thoroughfare Gap upon the railroad at Manassas would have been utterly impracticable. So confidently did I expect, from the assurances which I had time and again received, that these troops would be in position, or at all events, so far advanced toward me, that Jackson's movement toward White Plains and in the direction of Thoroughfare Gap, had caused but little uneasiness; but on the night of the 26th it was very apparent to me that all these expected reinforcements had utterly failed me; and that upon the small force under my own immediate command, I must depend alone for any present operations against the enemy.

It was easy for me to retire in the direction of the lower fords of the Rappahannock to Fredericksburg, so as to bring me in immediate contact with the forces there or arriving there; but by so doing I should have left open the whole front of Washington; and after my own disappointment of the reinforcements which I had expected, I was not sure that there was any sufficient force, in the absence of the army under my command, to cover the Capital. I determined, therefore, at once to abandon the line of the Rappahannock, and throw my whole force in the direction of Gainesville and Manassas Junction, to crush the enemy who had passed through Thoroughfare Gap, and to interpose between the army of Gen. Lee and Bull Run. During the night of the 26th the main body of the enemy still occupied their positions from Sulphur Springs to Waterloo Bridge and above; but toward morning on the 27th, I think their advance moved off in the direction of White Plains, pursuing the route previously

3

taken by Jackson, and, no doubt, with a view of uniting with him eastward of the Bull Run range.

From the 18th of August, until the morning of the 27th, the troops under my command had been continuously marching and fighting night and day, and during the whole of that time there was scarcely an interval of an hour without the roar of artillery. The men had had but little sleep, were greatly worn down with fatigue, had had little time to get proper food or to eat it, had been engaged in constant battles and skirmishes, and had performed services, laborious, dangerous and excessive, beyond any previous experience in this country. As was to be expected, under such circumstances, the numbers of the army under my command had been greatly reduced by death, by wounds, by sickness and by fatigue, so that on the morning of the 27th of August, I estimated my whole effective force (and I think the estimate was large) as follows: Sigel's Corps, 9,000, Banks' Corps, 5,000; McDowell's Corps, including Reynold's Division, 15,500; Reno's Corps, 7,000; the Corps of Heintzelman and Porter (the freshest, by far, in that army) about 18,000 men, making in all 54,500 men. Our cavalry numbered, on paper, about 4,000; but their horses were completely broken down, and there were not 500 men, all told, capable of doing such service as should be expected from cavalry. The Corps of Heintzelman had reached Warrenton Junction, but without wagons, without artillery, and with only forty rounds of ammunition to the man, and without even horses for the general and field officers. The Corps of Porter had also reached Warrenton Junction, with a very small supply of provisions, and but forty rounds of ammunition for each man.

On the morning of the 27th, in accordance with the purpose previously set forth, I directed McDowell to move forward rapidly on Gainesville, by the Warrenton Turnpike, with his own Corps, and Sigel's, and the Division of Reynolds', so as to reach that point during the night. I directed Gen. Reno, with his Corps, followed by Kearney's Division of Heintzelman's Corps, to move rapidly on Greenwich, so as to reach there that night; to communicate at once with Gen. McDowell, and to support him in any operations against the enemy in the vicinity of Gainesville. I moved forward along the railroad toward Manassas Junction with Hooker's Division of Heintzelman's Corps, leaving orders for Gen. Porter to remain with his Corps at Warrenton Junction until relieved by Gen. Banks, who was marching to that place from Fayetteville, and as soon as he was relieved to push forward also in the direction of Gainesville, where, at that time, I expected that the main collision with the enemy would occur.

The army trains of all the Corps I instructed to take the road to Warrenton Junction, and follow in the rear of Hooker's Division toward Manassas Junction, so that the road pursued by the trains was entirely covered from any possible interruption by the enemy. On the afternoon of the 27th a severe engagement occurred between Hooker's Division and Ewell's Division of Jackson's forces. The action commenced about four miles west of Bristow Station. Ewell was driven back along the railroad, but still confronted Hooker at dark along the banks of Broad Run, immediately in front of Bristow Station, at which point I arrived at sunset. The loss in this engagement was about three hundred killed and wounded on each side, the enemy leaving his dead, many of his wounded and much of his baggage on the field of battle.

The railroad had been torn up and the bridges burned in several places between Bristow Station and Warrenton Junction. I accordingly directed Maj.-Gen. Banks to cover the railroad trains at Warrenton Junction until Gen. Porter's Corps had marched from that place, and then to run back the trains as far as practicable, and, covering them with his troops, to repair the bridges as fast as possible. I also directed Capt. Merrill, of the engineers, with a considerable force, to repair the railroad track and bridges as far as possible in the direction of Bristow Station. The road was accordingly put in order from Warrenton Junction to Kettle Run, during the 27th, and the trains ran back to that point early next day. At dark on the 27th Gen. Hooker reported to me that his ammunition was nearly exhausted, that he had but five rounds to a man left. I had by that time become convinced that the whole force under Jackson, consisting of his own, A. P. Hill's and Ewell's Divisions, was south of the turnpike, and in the immediate neighborhood of Manassas Junction.

Gen. McDowell reached his position during the night of the 27th, as did also Kearney and Reno, and it was clear on that night that we had interposed completely between Jackson and the main body of the enemy, which was still west of the Bull Run range, and in the neighborhood of White Plains. Thinking it altogether likely that Jackson would mass his whole force and attempt to turn our right at Bristow Station, and knowing that Hooker, for want of ammunition, was in little condition to make long resistance, I sent back orders to Gen. Porter, about dark of the 27th, to move forward at 1 o'clock in the night, and report to me at Bristow by daylight in the morning, leaving instructions in some detail for Banks, who was expected at Warrenton Junction during that night or early in the morning. The orders for all these movements are herewith appended. Gen. Porter failed utterly to obey the orders that were sent to him; giving as an excuse that his men were tired, that they would straggle in the night, and that a wagon train, proceeding eastward, in the rear of Hooker's Division, would offer obstructions to his march. He, however, made no attempt whatever to comply with this order, although it was stated to him in the order itself that his presence was necessary on all accounts at daylight, and that the officer delivering the despatch was instructed to conduct him to the field.

There were but two courses left open to Jackson in consequence of this sudden and unexpected movement of the army. He could not retrace his steps through Gainesville, as it was occupied by McDowell, having at command a force equal, if not superior to his own. He was either obliged therefore to retreat through Centreville, which would carry him still further from the main body of Lee's army, or, to mass his forces, assault us at Bristow Station, and turn our right. He pursued the former course, and retired through Centreville. This mistake of Jackson's alone saved us from the serious consequences which would have followed this disobedience of orders on the part of Gen. Porter.

At nine o'clock on the night of the 27th, satisfied of Jackson's position, I sent orders to Gen. McDowell to push forward at the very earliest dawn of day, toward Manasses Junction from Gainesville, resting his right on the Manassas Gap Railroad, and throwing his left well to the east. I directed Gen. Reno to march at the same hour from Greenwich, direct upon Manasses Junction, and Kearney to march at the same hour upon Bristow. This latter order was sent to Kearney to render my right at Bristow perfectly secure against the probable movement of Jackson in that direction. Kearney arrived at Bristow about 8 o'clock in the morning. Reno being on the left, and marching direct upon Manasses Junction. I immediately pushed Kearney forward in pursuit of Ewell, toward Manassas, followed by Hooker. Gen. Porter's Corps did not arrive at Bristow until half-past ten o'clock in the morning; and the moment he found that Jackson had evacuated Manasses Junction, he requested permission to halt at Bristow, and rest his men. Syke's division of Porter's Corps, had spent the whole day of the 27th, from 10 o'clock in the morning, until daylight of the 28th, in camp at Warrenton Junction. Morrell's Division of the same Corps had arrived at Warrenton Junction during the day of the 27th, and also remained there during the whole of that night. Porter's Corps was by far the freshest in the whole army, and should have been, and, I believe, was, in better condition for service than any troops we had.

Gen. McDowell reported to me afterwards, that he had given orders for the movement of his command upon Manassas Junction at 2 o'clock at night, in accordance with the directions I had sent him, but that Gen. Sigel, who commanded his advance, and was at Gainesville, instead of moving forward from Gainesville at daylight, as he was ordered, was absolutely with his advance in that town as late as 7½ o'clock in the morning. Meantime, beginning about 3 o'clock in the morning of the 28th, Jackson commenced evacuating Manassas Junction, and his troops were marching from that point in the direction of Centreville, until 10 or 11 o'clock in the day. If the whole force under McDowell had moved forward as directed, and at the time specified, they would have intercepted Jackson's retreat toward Centreville by 8 o'clock in the morning, and I do not believe it would have been possible for Jackson to have crossed Bull Run, so closely engaged with our forces, without heavy loss. [See McDowell's report concerning the delay of Gen. Sigel.]

I reached Manassas Junction with Kearney's Division and Reno's Corps about 12 o'clock on the day of the 28th, less than an hour after Jackson in person had retired. I immediately pushed forward Hooker, Kearney, and Reno upon Centreville, and sent orders to Fitz John

Porter to come forward to Manassas Junction. I also wrote to Mc-Dowell, and stated the facts so far as we were then able to ascertain them, and directed him to call back the whole of his force, that had come in the direction of Manassas Junction, and to move forward upon Centreville. He had, however, without my knowledge, detached Ricketts' Division in the direction of Thoroughfare Gap, and that Division was no longer available in his movement towards Centreville.

Late in the afternoon of the 28th, Kearney drove the enemy's rear guard out of Centreville, and occupied that town, with his advance beyond it, about dark. The enemy retreated through Centreville, one portion of his force taking the road by Sudley Springs, and the other pursuing the Warrenton turnpike toward Gainesville, destroying the bridges on that road, over Bull Run and Cub Run; McDowell, with his whole force, consisting of his own Corps, (except Ricketts' Division,) Sigel's Corps, and the Division of Reynolds, marching in the direction of Centreville, encountered the advance of Jackson's force retreating toward Thoroughfare Gap, about 6 o'clock on the evening of the 28th. A severe action took place between King's Division, of McDowell's Corps, and the advance of Jackson, which was terminated by darkness. Each party maintained its ground. Gibbons' Brigade, of King's Division, which was in the advance of that Division, sustained the brunt of the action, but was supported handsomely by Doubleday's Brigade, which came into action shortly after. This engagement and its result, were reported to me near Centreville, about 10 o'clock that night.

I felt sure then, and so stated, that there was no escape for Jackson. I accordingly sent orders to Gen. McDowell, as also to Gen. King, several times during the night of the 29th, and once by his own Staff officer, to hold his ground at all hazards, and prevent the retreat of Jackson to the West, and that at daylight in the morning our whole force from Centreville and Manassas Junction would be up with the enemy, who must be crushed between us. I also sent orders to Gen. Kearney to push forward at 1 o'clock that night cautiously from Centreville along the Warrenton Turnpike, to drive in the pickets of the enemy, and to keep closely in contact with him during the night; to rest his left on the Warrenton Turnpike, and throw his right well to the north, if possible across Little River Turnpike; at daylight in the morning to assault vigorously with his right advance; and that Hooker and Reno would be up with him very shortly after daydawn. I sent orders to Gen. Porter, whom I supposed to be at Manassas Junction, where he should have been, in compliance with my orders of the day previous, to move upon Centreville at the earliest dawn, and stated to him the position of the forces, and that a severe battle would undoubtedly be fought during the morning of the 29th. The only apprehension I had at that time was, that Jackson might attempt to retreat to the north in the direction of Leesburg, and for the purpose of preventing this, I directed Kearney to keep closely in contact with him during the whole of the night of the 28th. My force was so disposed that McDowell, Sigel and Reynolds, whose joint forces amounted to about 25,000 men, were immediately west of Jackson, and between him and Thoroughfare Gap, while Kearney, Hooker, Reno and Porter, about 25,000 strong, were to fall on him from the east at daylight in the morning, or very shortly after. With this disposition of troops we were so far in advance of Longstreet, that by using our whole force vigorously, we should be able to crush Jackson before Longstreet could by any possibility reach the scene of action.

To my great disappointment, however, I learned, toward daylight, on the morning of the 29th, that King's Division had fallen back in the direction of Manassas Junction, thus leaving open the road to Thoroughfare Gap, and making new movements and dispositions of troops immediately necessary.

I submit herewith the reports of Gens. King, Gibbon and Doubleday, of the action of the evening of the 28th, as also a detailed report of Gen. McDowell. The orders directing all these movements are also appended, and they bring the operations of the army up to the 29th of August.

The losses in King's Division, in the action of the evening of the 28th, were principally in Gibbon's Brigade of that Division, and numbered ——.

Gibbon's Brigade consisted of some of the best troops in the service, and the conduct of both men and officers was gallant and distinguished. The report of Gen. King, herewith appended, exhibits his high opinion of the conduct of this Brigade, and of the officers who distinguished themselves in that action.

The disposition of the troops on the west of Jackson having failed through Ricketts' movement toward Thoroughfare Gap, and the consequent withdrawal of King, an immediate change in the disposition and proposed movements of the troops for the succeeding day became necessary; and about daylight on the morning of the 29th, shortly after I received information of the withdrawal of King's Division, I sent orders to Gen. Sigel, who was in the neighborhood of Groveton, supported by Reynolds' Division, to attack the enemy vigorously as soon as it was light enough to see and bring him to a stand, if it were possible for him to do so. I instructed Gen. Heintzelman to push forward from Centreville toward Gainesville at the earliest dawn, with the Divisions of Hooker and Kearney, and directed Gen. Reno to follow closely in his rear, to use all speed, and as soon as they came up with the enemy to establish communication with Sigel, and attack with the utmost promptness and vigor. I also sent orders to Maj.-Gen. Fitz John Porter, at Manassas Junction, to move forward with the utmost rapidity, with his own Corps and King's Division of McDowell's Corps, which was supposed to be at that point, upon Gainesville, by the direct road from Manassas Junction to that place. I urged him to make all speed, that he might come up with the enemy and be able to turn his flank near where the Warrenton Turnpike is intersected by the road from Manassas Junction to Gainesville. Shortly after sending this order, I received a note from Gen. McDowell, whom I had not been able to find during the night of the 28th, dated at Manassas Junction, requesting that King's Division might not be taken from his command. I immediately sent a joint order to Gens. McDowell and Porter, directing them, with their two Corps, to march with all speed toward Gainesville, on the direct road from Manassas Junction. This order, which is appended, sets forth in detail the movements they were directed to make.

Sigel attacked the enemy about daylight on the morning of the 29th, a mile or two east of Groveton, where he was soon joined by the Divisions of Hooker and Kearney. Jackson fell back several miles, but was so closely pressed by these forces that he was compelled to make a stand, and to make the best defense possible. He accordingly took up a position with his left in the neighborhood of Sudley Springs, his right a little to the south of Warrenton Turnpike, and his line covered by an old railroad grade which leads from Gainesville in the direction of Leesburg. His batteries, which were numerous, and some of them of heavy calibre, were posted behind the ridges in the open ground on both sides of Warrenton Turnpike, while the mass of his troops was sheltered in dense woods behind the railroad embankment.

I arrived on the field from Centreville about noon, and found the two armies confronting each other, both considerably cut up by the sharp action in which they had been engaged since daylight in the morning. Heintzelman's corps occupied the right of our line, in front or west of the Sudley Springs road. Gen. Sigel was on his left, with his line extended a short distance south of the Warrenton Turnpike; the division of Gen. Schenck occupying the high ground to the left of the road. The extreme left was occupied by Gen. Reynolds. Gen. Reno's Corps had reached the field, and the most of it had been pushed forward into action, leaving four regiments in reserve, and in rear of the centre of our line. Immediately after I reached the ground, Gen. Sigel reported to me that his line was weak; that the divisions of Schurz and Steinwehr were much cut up, and ought to be drawn back from the front. I informed Gen. Sigel that this was utterly impossible, as there were no troops to replace them, and that he must hold his ground; that I would not again push his troops into action, as the Corps of Porter and McDowell were moving forward from Manassas Junction, on the road to Gainesville, and must very soon be in position to fall upon the enemy's right flank, and probably upon his rear I rode to the front of our line, and inspected it from right to left, giving the same information to Gens. Heintzelman and Reno. The troops were accordingly suffered to rest in their positions, and to re-supply themselves with ammunition. From 12 until 4 o'clock very severe skirmishes occurred constantly at various points on our line, and were brought on at every indication the enemy made of a disposition to retreat.

About two o'clock in the afternoon several pieces of artillery were discharged on the extreme right of the enemy's line, and I fully believed that Gens. Porter and McDowell had reached their positions, and had become engaged with the enemy. I did not hear more than three shots fired, and was at a loss to know what had become of those two Corps, or what was delaying them, but I received information shortly afterward, that Gen. McDowell was advancing to join the main body by the Sudley Springs road, and would probably be up with us in two hours. At half-past 4 o'clock, I sent a peremptory order to Gen. Porter to push forward at once, into action on the enemy's right, and if possible to turn his rear, stating to him generally, the condition of things on the field in front of me. About 5½ o'clock, when Gen. Porter should have been coming into action in compliance with this order, I directed Gens. Heintzelman and Reno to attack the enemy. The attack was made with great gallantry, and the whole of the left of the enemy was doubled back toward his centre, and our own forces, after a sharp conflict of an hour and a half, occupied the field of battle, with the dead and wounded of the enemy in our hands. In this attack, Grover's brigade of Hooker's Division was particularly distinguished by a determined bayonet charge, breaking two of the enemy's lines, and penetrating to the third before it could be checked. By this time Gen. McDowell had arrived on the field, and I pushed his Corps immediately to the front, along the Warrenton turnpike, with orders to fall upon the enemy, who was retreating towards the pike from the direction of Sudley Springs. The attack along the turnpike was made by King's Division at about sunset in the evening; but by that time the advance of the main body of the enemy under Longstreet, had begun to reach the field, and King's Division encountered a stubborn and determined resistance at a point about three-fourths of a mile in front of our line of battle.

While this attack was going on, the forces of Heintzelman and Reno continued to push back the left of the enemy in the direction of Warrenton Turnpike, so that about 8 o'clock in the evening the greater portion of the field of battle was occupied by our army. Nothing was heard of Gen. Porter up to that time, and his forces took no part whatever in the action, but were suffered by him to lie idle on their arms, within sight and sound of the battle during the whole day. So far as I know, he made no effort whatever to comply with my orders or to take any part in the action. I do not hesitate to say that if he had discharged his duty as became a soldier under the circumstances, and had made a vigorous attack on the enemy as he was expected and directed to do, at any time up to 8 o'clock that night, we should have utterly crushed or captured the larger portion of Jackson's force before he could have been by any possibility sufficiently reinforced to have made an effective resistance. I did not myself feel for a moment that it was necessary for me, having given Gen. Porter an order to march toward the enemy, in a particular direction, to send him in addition specific orders to attack, it being his clear duty, and in accordance with every military precept, to have brought his forces into action wherever he encountered the enemy, when a furious battle with that enemy was raging during the whole day in his immediate presence. I believe, in fact I am positive, that at 5 o'clock on the afternoon of the 29th, Gen. Porter had in his front no considerable body of the enemy. I believed then, as I am very sure now, that it was easily practicable for him to have turned the right flank of Jackson, and to have fallen upon his rear; that if he had done so, we should have gained a decisive victory over the army under Jackson before he could have been joined by any of the forces of Longstreet, and that the army of Gen. Lee would have been so crippled and checked by the destruction of this large force as to have been no longer in condition to prosecute further operations of an aggressive character.

Our losses during the 29th were very heavy, but no separate return of killed and wounded for that day have been made to me. I believe, from all I could learn from Corps commanders, and so. reported, that our loss during that day was not less than six or eight thousand killed and wounded, and I think the estimate will be confirmed by the general reports, which cover the losses during the battles of the 27th, 28th, 29th and 30th August, and the 1st of September. My estimate of the loss of the enemy, reported to the Department on the morning of the 30th, was based upon the statements made to me by Gens. Hooker and Kearney, who had been over the whole field on the left. Gen. Hooker estimated the loss of the enemy as at least two to one, and Gen. Kearney as at least three to one of our own.

Every indication, during the night of the 29th and up to 10 o'clock on the morning of the 30th, pointed to the retreat of the enemy from our front. Paroled prisoners of our own, taken on the evening of the 29th, and who came into our lines on the morning of the 30th, reported the enemy retreating during the whole night in the direction of and along the Warrenton Turnpike. Gens. McDowell and Heintzelman, who reconnoitred the positions held by the enemy's left on the evening of the 29th, confirmed this statement. They reported to me that the positions occupied by the enemy's left had been evacuated, and that there was every indication that he was retreating in the direction of Gainesville.

On the morning of the 30th, as may be supposed, our troops, who had been so continually marching and fighting for so many days, were in a state of great exhaustion. They had had little to eat for two days previous, and artillery and cavalry horses had been in harness and saddled continuously for ten days, and had had no forage for two days previous. It may easily be imagined how little these troops, after such severe labors, and after undergoing such hardships and privation, were in condition for active and efficient service. I had telegraphed to the General-in-Chief on the 28th our condition, and had begged of him to have rations and forage sent forward to us from Alexandria with all dispatch. I informed him of the imminent need of cavalry horses to enable the cavalry belonging to the army to perform any service whatever. About daylight of the 30th I received a note from Gen. Franklin—herewith appended—written by direction of Gen. McClellan, and dated at 8 o'clock P. M. on the 29th, informing me that rations and forage would be loaded into the available wagons and

4

cars at Alexandria, as soon as I would send back a cavalry escort to bring out the trains. Such a letter, when we were fighting the enemy, and Alexandria was swarming with troops, needs no comment. Bad as was the condition of our cavalry, I was in no situation to spare troops from the front, nor could they have gone to Alexandria and returned within the time by which we must have had provisions or have fallen back in the direction of Washington. Nor do I yet see what service cavalry could have rendered in guarding railroad trains. It was not until I received this letter that I began to feel discouraged and nearly hopeless of any successful issue to the operations with which I was charged; but I felt it to be my duty, notwithstanding the desperate condition of my command, from great fatigue, from want of provisions and forage, and from the small hope that I had of any effective assistance from Alexandria, to hold my position at all hazards and under all privations, unless overwhelmed by the superior forces of the enemy. I had received no sort of information of any troops coming forward to my assistance since the 24th, and did not expect, on the morning of the 30th, that any assistance would reach me from the direction of Washington; but I determined again to give battle to the enemy on the 30th, and at least to lay on such blows as would cripple him as much as possible, and delay as long as practicable any further advance toward the Capital. I accordingly prepared to renew the engagement.

At that time my effective forces, greatly reduced by losses in killed, wounded, missing and broken down men, during the severe operations of the two or three days and nights previous; the sharp actions of Hooker, King and Ricketts on the 27th and 28th, and the furious battle on the 29th, were estimated by me and others as follows: McDowell's Corps, including Reynolds' Division, 12,000 men; Sigel's Corps, 7,000; Reno's Corps 7,000; Heintzelman's Corps 7,000; Porter's Corps, which had been in no engagement, and was, or ought to have been, perfectly fresh, I estimated at about 12,000 men, including the Brigade of Piatt, which formed a part of Sturgis' Division, and the only portion that ever joined me. But of this force the Brigades of Piatt and Griffin, numbering, as I understood, about 5,000 men had been suffered to march off at daylight on the 30th for Centreville, and were not available for operations on that day. This reduced Porter's effective force in the field to about 7,000 men, which gave me a total force of 40,000 men. Banks' Corps, about 5,000 strong, was at Bristow Station, in charge of the railroad trains, and of a portion of the wagon trains of the army, still at that place.

Between 12 and 2 o'clock in the day I advanced the Corps of Porter, supported by King's Division of McDowell's Corps, to attack the enemy along the Warrenton Turnpike; at the same time I directed Heintzelman and Reno, on our right, to push forward to the left and front toward Warrenton Turnpike, and attack the enemy's left in flank if possible. For a short time Ricketts' Division of McDowell's Corps was placed in support of this movement on our right.

It was necessary for me to act thus promptly, and make the attack, as I had not the time, for want of provisions and forage, to await an attack from the enemy, nor did I think it policy to so do under the circumstances. During the whole night of the 29th, and the morning of the 30th, the advance of the main army, under Lee, was arriving on the field to reinforce Jackson, so that by 12 or 1 o'clock in the day, we were confronted by forces greatly superior to our own ; and these forces were being every moment largely increased by fresh arrivals of the enemy from the direction of Thoroughfare Gap. Every moment of delay increased the odds against us, and I therefore advanced to the attack as rapidly as I was able to bring my forces into action. Shortly after Gen. Porter moved forward to the attack by the Warrenton Turnpike, and the assault on the enemy was begun by Heintzelman and Reno on the right, it became apparent that the enemy was massing his troops, as fast as they arrived on the field, on his right and was moving forward from that direction to turn our left; at which point it was plain he intended to make his main attack. I accordingly directed Gen. McDowell to recall Ricketts' Division immediately from our right, and post it on the left of our line. The attack of Porter was neither vigorous nor persistent, and his troops soon retired in considerable confusion. As soon as they commenced to fall back, the enemy advanced to the assault, and our whole line, from right to left, was soon furiously engaged. The main attack of the enemy was made upon our left, but was met with stubborn resistance by the Divisions of Gen. Schenck, Gen. Milroy and Gen. Reynolds, who, shortly after the action began, were reinforced on the left and rear by the whole of Ricketts' Division. The action raged furiously for several hours, the enemy bringing up his heavy reserves, and pouring mass after mass of his troops upon our left. So greatly superior in number were his forces, that, while overpowering us on our left, he was able to assault us also with superior forces on our right. Porter's forces were rallied and brought to a halt as they were retiring to the rear. As soon as they could be used, I pushed them forward to support our left, and they there rendered distinguished service, especially the Brigade of regulars under Col. Buchanan.

Tower's Brigade of Ricketts' Division was pushed forward into action in support of Reynolds' Division, and was led forward in person by Gen. Tower with conspicuous skill and gallantry. The conduct of that Brigade, in plain view of all the forces on our left, was especially distinguished, and drew forth hearty and enthusiastic cheers. The example of this Brigade was of great service, and infused new spirit into all the troops who witnessed its intrepid conduct. Reno's Corps was also withdrawn from its position on our right centre late in the afternoon, and was thrown into action on our left, where it behaved with conspicuous gallantry.

Notwithstanding these great disadvantages, our troops held their ground with the utmost firmness and obstinacy. The loss on both sides was very heavy. By dark our left had been forced back about half or three-quarters of a mile, but still remained firm and unbroken, and still covered the turnpike in our rear.

About 6 o'clock in the afternoon I heard accidentally that Franklin's Corps had arrived at a point about four miles east of Centreville, and twelve miles in our rear, and that it was only about 8,000 strong.

The result of the battle of the 30th, the very heavy losses we had suffered, and the complete prostration of our troops from hunger and fatigue, made it plain to me that we were no longer able, in the face of such overwhelming odds, to maintain our position so far to the front; nor could we have been able to do so under any circumstances, suffering, as were the men and horses from fatigue and hunger, and weakened by the heavy losses incident to the uncommon hardships which they had suffered.

About eight o'clock at night, therefore, I sent written instructions to the commanders of Corps to withdraw leisurely towards Centreville, and stated to them what route each should pursue, and where they should take post. Gen. Reno was instructed, with his whole Corps, to cover the movement of the army toward Centreville. The withdrawal was made slowly, quietly and in good order, no pursuit whatever having been attempted by the enemy. A division of infantry, with its batteries, was posted to cover the crossing at Cub Run.

The exact losses in this battle I am unable to give, as the reports received from the Corps commanders only exhibit the aggregate losses during the whole of the operations from August 22d to September 2d. Before leaving the field that night, I sent orders to Gen. Banks, at Bristow Station, to destroy the railroad trains and such of the stores in them as he was unable to carry off, and join me at Centreville. I had previously sent him orders to throw into each wagon of the army trains as much as possible of the stores from the railroad cars, and to be sure and bring off with him, from Warrenton Junction and Bristow Station, all the ammunition, and all the sick and wounded that could be transported, and for this purpose, if it were necessary, to throw out the personal baggage, tents, &c., from the regimental trains. These several orders are appended. At no time during August 28, 29, 30 and 31, was the road between Bristow Station and Centreville interrupted by the enemy. The whole of the trains of the army were on that road, in charge of Gen. Banks, and covered and protected by his whole Corps. If any of these wagons were lost, as I believe none were, it was wholly without necessity. I enter thus specifically into this matter, and submit the orders sent to Gen. Banks, and his subsequent report to me, because no part of the misrepresentation of this campaign has been greater than the statement of our heavy loss of wagons and supplies. The orders submitted will show conclusively that every arrangement was made, in the utmost detail, for the security of our trains and supplies, and I am quite convinced that Gen. Banks is not the man to neglect the duty with which he was charged.

I arrived at Centreville between 9 and 10 o'clock on the night of the 30th. On the same night I sent orders to the Corps commanders to report to me in person as early after daylight as possible on the morning of the 31st, and on that morning the troops were directed to be posted as follows: Porter was to occupy the entrenchments on the north or right of Centreville; Franklin on his left in the intrenchments; in rear of Centreville, between Franklin and Porter, as a support, was posted the Corps of Heintzelman; Sigel occupied the intrenchments on the left and south side of the town, with Reno on his left and rear. Banks was ordered to take post as soon as he arrived, on the north side of Bull Run, and to cover the bridge on the road from Centreville to Manassas Junction; Sumner, as soon as he arrived, was ordered to take post between Centreville and Chantilly, and to occupy Chantilly in force; McDowell was posted about two miles in the rear of Centreville, on the road to Fairfax Court House. Ammunition trains and some provisions were gotten up on the 31st, and all Corps commanders were notified, by special orders to each, that the ammunition trains were parked immediately in the rear of Centreville, and were directed to send officers to procure such ammunition as was needed in their respective Corps. I directed the whole of the trains of the army to be unloaded at Centreville, and sent to Fairfax Station to bring up forage and rations.

We remained during the whole day of the 31st resting the men, getting up supplies of provisions, and resupplying the commands with ammunition.

The enemy's cavalry appeared in force in front of our advance at Cub Run, during the morning of the 31st, but made no attempt to cross, and no attack upon our troops posted there. A few pieces of artillery were fired, but with no result on either side.

The whole force that I had at Centreville, as reported to me by the Corps commanders, on the morning of the 1st of September, after receiving the Corps of Sumner and Franklin, was as follows: McDowell's Corps, 10,000 men; Sigel's Corps, about 7,000; Heintzelman's Corps, about 6,000; Reno's, 6,000; Banks', 5,000; Sumner's, 11,000; Porter's 10,000; Franklin's 8,000—in all 63,000 men. From these forces two Brigades, as I before stated, had been sent to Fairfax Station, to guard the trains and the depot at that place, which makes it necessary to deduct 4,000 men. It is proper for me to state here, and I do it with regret and reluctance, that at least one-half of this great diminution of our forces was occasioned by skulking and straggling from the army. The troops which were brought into action fought with gallantry and determination, but thousands of men straggled away from their commands, and were not in any action. I had posted several regiments in rear of the field of battle, on the 29th of August, and although many thousand stragglers and skulkers were arrested by them, many others passed around through the woods, and did not rejoin their commands during the remainder of the campaign. I had telegraphed to the General-in-Chief, from Rappahannock Station, on the 22d, that this practice of straggling was very common, and was reducing our force considerably even at that time. I also sent orders on the same day to Gen. Sturgis, to arrest all stragglers arriving in Alexandria; to confine them in military prisons, and to bring them to speedy trial. The active and incessant movements of the army prevented me, during the whole of this campaign, from giving that attention to the subject, except in orders, which ought to be and must be given to it, to preserve efficiency and discipline among any troops. Our cavalry at Centreville was completely broken down, no horses whatever having reached us to remount it. Gens. Buford and Bayard, commanding the whole of the cavalry force of the army, reported to me that there were not five horses to the company that could be forced into a trot. It was impossible, therefore, to cover our front with cavalry, or to make cavalry reconnoissances, as is usual and necessary in front of an army.

I directed Gen. Sumner, on the morning of the 1st of September, to push forward a reconnoissance of two Brigades toward the Little River Turnpike, to ascertain if the enemy were making any movements in the direction of Germantown or Fairfax Court House. The enemy was found moving again slowly toward our right; heavy columns of his forces being in march toward Fairfax along Little River Pike. The main body of our forces was so much broken down and so completely exhausted, that they were in no condition, even on the 1st of September, for any active operations against the enemy; but I determined to attack at daylight on the 2d of September, in front of Chantilly. The movement of the enemy had become so developed by the afternoon of the 1st, and was so evidently directed at Fairfax Court House, with a view of turning my right, that I made the necessary disposition of troops to fight a battle between the Little River Pike and the road from Centreville to Fairfax Court House. I sent Gen. Hooker early in the afternoon to Fairfax Court House, and directed him to assemble all the troops that were in the vicinity, and to push forward to Germantown with his advance. I directed McDowell to move back along the road to Fairfax Court House, as far as Difficult Creek, and to connect by his right with Hooker. Reno was to push forward to the north of the road from Centreville to Fairfax, in the direction of Chantilly. Heintzelman's Corps was directed to take post on the road between Centreville and Fairfax, immediately in the rear of Reno. Franklin took post on McDowell's left and rear; Sumner was posted on the left of Heintzelman, while the Corps of Sigel and Porter were directed to unite with the right of Sumner; Banks was instructed with the wagon trains of the army to pursue the old Braddock road and come into the Alexandria turnpike in the rear of Fairfax Court House. Just before sunset on the 1st the enemy attacked us on our right, but was met by Hooker, McDowell, Reno, and Kearney's Division of Heintzelman's Corps. A very severe action occurred in the midst of a terrific thunder storm, and was terminated shortly after dark. The enemy was driven back entirely from our front, but during that engagement we lost two of our best, and one of our most distinguished officers—Maj.-Gen. Kearney and Brig.-Gen. Stevens—who were both killed while gallantly leading their commands, and in front of their line of battle. It is unnecessary for me to say one word in commendation of two officers who were so well and widely known to the country. Words cannot express my sense of the zeal, the gallantry and the sympathy of that most earnest and accomplished soldier, Maj.-Gen. Kearney. In him the country has suffered a loss which it will be difficult, if not impossible, to repair. He died as he would have wished to die, and as became his heroic character.

On the morning of the 2d of September, the enemy still continuing his movements toward our right, my whole force was posted behind Difficult Creek, from Flint Hill to the Alexandria turnpike. Although we were quite able to maintain our position at that place until the stragglers could be collected, and the army, after its labors and perils, put into condition for effective service, I considered it advisable, for reasons which developed themselves at Centreville, were communicated to the General-in-Chief, and are set forth herewith in the appendix, that the troops should be drawn back to the intrenchments in front of Washington, and that some reorganization should be made of them, in order that earlier effective service should be secured than was possible in their condition at that time. I received orders about 12 o'clock on the 2d of September to draw back the forces within the intrenchments, which was done in good order, and without any interruption by the enemy.

The reasons which induced me, before I took the field in Virginia, to express to the Government my desire to be relieved from the command of the Army of Virginia, and to return to the West, existed in equal, if not greater force, at this time than when I first stated them. I accordingly renewed urgently my application to be relieved. The Government assented to it with some reluctance, and I was transferred to the Department of the Northwest, for which Department I left Washington on the the 7th of September.

It seems proper for me, since so much misrepresentation has been put into circulation as to the support I received from the Army of the Potomac, to state precisely what forces of that army came under my command, and were at any time engaged in the active operations of the campaign. Reynolds' Division of Pennsylvania reserves, about 2,500 joined me on the 23d of August, at Rappahannock Station. The Corps of Heintzelman and Porter, about 18,000 strong, joined me on the 26th and 27th of August, at Warrenton Junction. The Pennsylvania reserves, under Reynolds, and Heintzelman's Corps, consisting of the Divisions of Hooker and Kearney, rendered most gallant and efficient service in all the operations which occurred after they had reported to me. Porter's Corps, from unnecessary and unusual delays, and frequent and flagrant disregard of my orders, took no part whatever except in the action of the 30th of August. This small fraction of 20,500 men was all of the 91,000 veteran troops from Harrison's Landing, which ever drew trigger under my command, or in any way took part in that campaign. By the time the Corps of Franklin and Sumner, 19,000 strong, joined me at Centreville, the original army of Virginia, as well as the Corps of Heintzelman, and the Division of Reynolds, had been so much cut up in the severe actions in which they had been engaged, and were so much broken down and diminished in numbers by the constant and excessive duties they had performed, that they were in little condition for any effective service whatever, and required and should have had some days of rest to put them in anything like condition to perform their duties in the field.

Such is the history of a campaign, substantiated by documents written during the operations, and hereto appended, which has been misunderstood to an extent perhaps, unparalleled in the history of warfare. I submit it here to the public judgment, with all confidence that it will be fairly and deliberately considered, and a just verdict pronounced upon it, and upon the army engaged in it. Upon such unbiased judgment I am very willing (setting aside any previous record I have made during the war) to rest my reputation as a soldier. I shall submit cheerfully to the verdict of my countrymen; but I desire that that verdict shall be rendered upon a full knowledge of the facts.

I well understood, as does every military man, how difficult and how thankless was the duty devolved upon me; and I am not ashamed to say that I would gladly have avoided it if I could have done so consistently with my sense of duty to the Government. To confront with a small army vastly superior forces; to fight battles without hope of victory, but only to gain time, and to embarrass and delay the forward movement of the enemy, is of all duties the most hazardous and the most difficult that can be imposed upon any General or any army. While such operations require the highest courage and endurance on the part of the troops, they are, perhaps, unlikely to be understood or appreciated, and the results, however successful, have little in them to attract popular attention and applause.

At no time could I have hoped to fight a successful battle with the immensely superior force of the enemy which confronted me, and which was able at any time to outflank me and bear my small army to the dust. It was only by constant movement, by incessant watchfulness and hazardous skirmishes and battles that the forces under my command were not overwhelmed, while at the same time the enemy was embarrassed and delayed in his advance upon Washington until the forces from the Peninsula were *at length* assembled for the defence of the city. I did hope that, in the course of these operations the enemy might commit some imprudence or leave some opening, of which I could take such advantage as to gain at least a partial victory over his forces. This opportunity was presented by the advance of Jackson upon Manassas Junction; but, although the best dispositions possible under the circumstances, were ordered, the object was frustrated in a manner and by causes which are now well understood. I am gratified to know that the conduct of the campaign, every detail of which was communicated, day by day, to the General-in-Chief, was fully approved by him and by the Government, and I now gladly submit the subject to the judgment of the country.

Gen. Banks rendered most efficient and faithful service throughout the campaign, and his conduct at the battle of Cedar Mountain, and the operations on the Upper Rappahannock, was marked by great coolness, intrepidity and zeal. Gen. McDowell led his Corps during the whole campaign with ability and vigor, and I am greatly indebted to him for zealous and distinguished service, both in the battles of the 29th and 30th of August, and in the operations which preceded and succeeded those battles. Gen. Sigel rendered useful service in reorganizing and putting in condition the First Army Corps of the Army of Virginia, and made many valuable and highly important reconnoissances during the operations of the campaign. I cannot express myself too highly of the zealous, gallant and cheerful manner in which Gen. Reno deported himself from the beginning to the end of the operations. Ever prompt, earnest and soldierly, he was the model of an accomplished soldier and gallant gentleman, and his loss has been a heavy blow to the army and to the country.

Gen. Heintzelman performed his duty faithfully and honestly, while the commanders of the Divisions of his Corps (Gens. Kearney and Hooker,) have that place in the public estimation which they have earned by many gallant and heroic actions and which renders it unnecessary for me to do aught except pay this tribute to the memory of one and to the rising fame of the other. Gens. Williams, Auger, Crawford, Green, Geary, Carroll and Prince, of Banks' Corps, have been already noticed for their gallant and distinguished conduct at Cedar Mountain. Gens. King and Ricketts, of McDowell's Corps led their Divisions throughout the operations, with skill and efficiency, and Gen. King, before he marched from Fredericksburg, rendered important service in organizing and dispatching the expeditions which, on several occasions, broke up the line of the Virginia Central Railroad. Gens. Patrick, Doubleday, Gibbon, Hartsuff, Duryea and Tower commanded their Brigades in the various operations of the campaign, with ability and zeal. The last named officer especially was particularly distinguished by the long marches which he made, by his untiring activity, and by the distinguished gallantry he displayed in the action of the 30th of August, in which action he was severely wounded at the head of his Brigade. Gen. Hatch, after being relieved from the command of the cavalry of Banks' Corps, was assigned to the command of an infantry brigade in King's Division of McDowell's Corps, and during part of the operations was in command of that Division, and rendered good service. Gens. Schenck and Milroy, of Sigel's Corps, exhibited great gallantry and zeal throughout the operations. They were engaged actively in the battles of the 29th and 30th of August, and their commands were among the last to leave the field of battle on the night of the 30th, Gen. Schenck being severely wounded on that day.

I must also mention in high terms the conduct of Gens. Schurz, Stahl and Steinwehr, during the actions of the 29th and 30th. Gens. Birney, Robinson and Grover, of Heintzelman's Corps, commanded their Brigades during the actions of the 29th and 30th, and Birney during the action of the 1st of September, with zeal and gallantry, and Gens. Birney and Grover were especially distinguished in

5

the actions of the 29th and 30th of August, and Birney also in the engagement of the 1st of September.

Gen. Stevens, of Reno's Corps, was zealous and active throughout the operations, and distinguished himself in the most conspicuous manner during the battles of the 29th and 30th of August. He was killed at the head of his command in the battle near Chantilly on the 1st September, and his death will be deeply felt by the army and the country. Lieut.-Col. R. C. Buchannan, commanding a brigade of regulars of Porter's Corps, was noticeable for distinguished service in the afternoon of the 30th of August. Of the conduct of the other officers commanding divisions or brigades of Porter's Corps, I know nothing, having received no report from that officer of the operations of his Corps. Brig. Gen. John F. Reynolds, commanding the Pennsylvania Reserves, merits the highest commendation at my hands. Prompt, active, and energetic, he commanded his division with distinguished ability throughout the operations, and performed his duties in all situations with zeal and fidelity. Gens. Seymour and Meade, of that division, in like manner performed their duties with ability and gallantary, and in all fidelity to the Government and to the army. Gen. Sturgis arrived at Warrenton Junction on the 26th of August, with Piatt's Brigade of his Division, the only portion of that Division which ever joined me. This Brigade was temporarily attached to the army Corps of Fitz John Porter, and although misled in consequence of orders to follow Griffin's Brigade of that Corps, which, for some unexplained reason, strayed from its Corps to Centreville on the 30th of August, was led forward from that place by Gens. Sturgis and Piatt as soon as it was discovered that Griffin did not intend to go forward to the field of battle, and reported to me late in the afternoon of that day. Shortly afterward the Brigade was thrown forward into action on our left, where they acquitted themselves with great courage. Brig.-Gen. Sturgis, as well as Gen. Piatt, deserve especial mention for the soldierly feeling which induced them, after being thus misled, and with the bad example of Griffin before their eyes, to push forward with such zeal and alacrity to the field of battle, and for the valuable services which they rendered in the action of the 30th of August. Gens. Bayard and Buford commanded all of the cavalry belonging to the Army of Virginia. Their duties were peculiarly arduous and hazardous, and it is not too much to say, that throughout the operations, from the first to the last day of the campaign, scarce a day passed that these officers did not render services which entitle them to the gratitude of the Government. The detachment of the signal Corps with the various army Corps rendered most important service, and I cannot speak too highly of the value of that Corps, and of the important information which, from time to time, they communicated to me. They were many times in positions of extreme peril, but were always prompt, and ready to encounter any danger in the discharge of their duties. Brig. Gen. Julius White, with one Brigade, was in the beginning of the campaign placed in command at Winchester. He was selected for that position because I felt entire confidence in his courage and ability, and during the whole of his service there, he performed his duty with the utmost efficiency, and relieved me entirely from any apprehension concerning that region of country. He was withdrawn from his position by orders direct from Washington, and passed from under my command. I transmit herewith reports of Corps, Division, and Brigade commanders, which will be found to embrace all the details of their respective operations, and which do justice to the officers and soldiers under their command. To my personal staff I owe much gratitude and many thanks. Their duties were particularly arduous, and at times led them into the midst of the various actions in which we were engaged. It is saying little when I state that they were zealous, untiring, and efficient throughout the campaign.

To Brig.-Gen. Roberts, in particular, I am indebted for services marked throughout by skill, courage, and unerring judgment, and worthy of the solid reputation as a soldier he has acquired by many years of previous faithful and distinguished military service. I desire, also, especially to mention Brig.-Gen. Elliott, Surgeon McParlin, Col. Beckwith, Lieut. Col. T. C. H. Smith, Capt. Piper, Chief of Artillery, Capt. Merrill of the Engineers, and Lieut. Schunk, Chief of Ordinance. I must also honorably mention the following members of my staff, the conduct of all of whom met my hearty approval, and merits high commendation: Cols. Macomb, Clary, Marshall, Butler, Morgan, and Welch; Majors Selfridge, and Meline; Capts. Asch, Douglas Pope, Haight, Atcheson, De Kay, Piatt, Paine, and Strother. Mr. McCain, confidential telegraph operator at my head quarters, accompanied me throughout the campaign, and was at all times eminently useful and efficient. My personal escort, consisting of two small companies of the First Ohio Cavalry, numbering about one hundred men, performed more arduous service, probably, than any troops in the campaign. As orderlies, messengers, and guards they passed many sleepless nights and weary days. Their conduct in all the operations, as in every battle, was marked by uncommon activity and gallantry. The reports of Corps, Divisions, and Brigade commanders, herewith submitted, exhibit the loss in killed, wounded, and missing in their respective commands. No report of any description has been received from the army Corps of Banks and Reno.

I am, General, respectfully, your obedient servant,

JNO. POPE, Major General.

Brig.-Gen. G. W. Cullum, Chief of Staff and Engineers, Headquarters of the Army.

APPENDIX.

[Copies of such of the Dispatches and Orders sent and received during the Campaign of the Army of Virginia as are referred to in the body of the Report, and are necessary to explain in detail the operations of that campaign.]

HEADQUARTERS ARMY OF VIRGINIA, }
Washington, July 18, 1862. }

General Orders No. 5.—Hereafter, as far as practicable, the troops of this command will subsist upon the country in which their operations are carried on. In all cases supplies for this purpose will be taken by the officers to whose department they properly belong, under the orders of the commanding officer of the troops for whose use they are intended. Vouchers will be given to the owners, stating on their face that they will be payable at the conclusion of the war, upon sufficient testimony being furnished that such owners have been loyal citizens of the United States since the date of the vouchers. Whenever it is known that supplies can be furnished in any district of the country where the troops are to operate, the use of trains for carrying subsistence will be dispensed with as far as possible.

By Command of Maj.-Gen. Pope.

Geo. D. Ruggles, Col., A. A. G. and Chief of Staff.
Official: T. C. H. Smith, Lt.-Col. and A. D. C.

HEADQUARTERS ARMY OF VIRGINIA, }
Washington, July 18, 1862. }

General Orders No. 6.—Hereafter, in any operations of the cavalry forces in this command, no supply nor baggage trains of any description will be used, unless so stated specially in the order for the movement. Two days cooked rations will be carried on the persons of the men, and all villages or neighborhoods through which they pass will be laid under contribution in the manner specified by General Orders No. 5, current series, from these headquarters, for the subsistence of men and horses. Movements of cavalry must always be made with celerity, and no delay in such movements will be excused hereafter on any pretext.

Whenever the order for the movement of any portion of this army emanates from these headquarters, the time of marching and that to be consumed in the execution of the duty will be specifically designated, and no departure therefrom will be permitted to pass unnoticed without the gravest and most conclusive reasons.

Commanding officers will be held responsible for strict and prompt compliance with every provision of this order.

By command of Maj.-Gen. Pope.

Geo. D. Ruggles, Col., A. A. G., and Chief of Staff.

Official: T. C. H. Smith, Lt.-Col. and A. D. C.

HEADQUARTERS ARMY OF VIRGINIA, }
Washington, July 20, 1862. }

General Orders No. 7.—The people of the Valley of the Shenandoah, and throughout the region of operations of this Army, living along the lines of railroad and telegraph, and along the routes of travel in rear of the United States forces, are notified that they will be held responsible for any injury done to the track, line or road, or for any attacks upon trains or straggling soldiers by bands of guerrillas in their neighborhood. No privileges and immunities of warfare apply to lawless bands of individuals not forming part of the organized forces of the enemy nor wearing the garb of soldiers, who, seeking and obtaining safety on pretext of being peaceful citizens, steal out in rear of the Army, attack and murder straggling soldiers, molest trains of supplies, destroy railroads, telegraph lines and bridges, and commit outrages disgraceful to civilized people and revolting to humanity. Evil disposed persons in rear of our armies, who do not themselves engage directly in these lawless acts, encourage them by refusing to interfere or to give any information by which such acts can be prevented, or the perpetrators punished.

Safety of life and property of all persons living in the rear of our advancing armies depends upon the maintenance of peace and quiet among themselves, and of the unmolested movement through their midst of all pertaining to the military service. They are to understand distinctly that this security of travel is their only warrant of personal safety.

It is therefore ordered, that wherever a railroad, wagon road, or telegraph, is injured by parties of guerrillas, the citizens living within five miles of the spot shall be turned out in mass to repair the damage, and shall, besides, pay to the United States, in money or in property, to be levied by military force, the full amount of the pay and subsistence of the whole force necessary to coerce the performance of the work during the time occupied in completing it.

If a soldier or legitimate follower of the Army be fired upon from any house, the house shall be razed to the ground, and the inhabitants sent prisoners to the headquarters of this Army. If such an outrage occur at any place distant from settlements, the people within five miles around shall be held accountable and made to pay an indemnity sufficient for the case.

Any persons detected in such outrages, either during the act or at any time afterward, shall be shot without awaiting civil process.

No such acts can influence the result of this war, and they can only lead to heavy afflictions to the population to no purpose.

It is therefore enjoined upon all persons, both for the security of their property and the safety of their own persons, that they act vigorously and cordially together to prevent the perpetration of such outrages.

While it is the wish of the General commanding this Army that all peaceably disposed persons who remain at their homes and pursue their accustomed avocations shall be subjected to no improper burden of war, yet their own safety must, of necessity, depend upon the strict preservation of peace and order among themselves, and they are to understand that nothing will deter him from enforcing promptly and to the full extent, every provision of this order.

By command of Maj.-Gen. Pope.

Geo. D. Ruggles, Col., A. A. G., and Chief of Staff.
Official : Lt. Col. Smith, Aid-de-Camp.

HEADQUARTERS ARMY OF VIRGINIA, }
Washington, July 23, 1863. }

General Orders, No. **11.**—Commanders of Army Corps, Divisions, Brigades, and detached commands, will proceed immediately to arrest all disloyal male citizens within their lines, or within their reach, in rear of their respective stations.

Such as are willing to take the oath of allegiance to the United States, and will furnish sufficient security for its observance, shall be permitted to remain at their homes, and pursue, in good faith their accustomed avocations.

Those who refuse shall be conducted South, beyond the extreme pickets of this army, and be notified that if found again anywhere within our lines, or at any point in rear, they will be considered spies, and subjected to the extreme rigor of military law.

If any person, having taken the oath of allegiance, as above specified, be found to have violated it, he shall be shot, and his property seized and applied to the public use.

All communication with any persons whatever, living within the lines of the enemy, is positively prohibited, except through the military authorities, and in the manner specified by military law; and any person concerned in writing or in carrying letters or messages in any other way, will be considered and treated as a spy within the lines of the United States Army.

By command of Major-Gen. Pope.

Geo. D. Ruggles, Col. A. A. G., and Chief of Staff.
Official : T. C. H. Smith, Lieut.-Col., and A. D. C.

HEADQUARTERS ARMY OF VIRGINIA, }
Near Sperryville, Va., Aug. 6, 1862. }

General Orders, No. **13.**—Hereafter, in all marches of the Army, no straggling, or lagging behind, will be allowed. Commanders of regiments will be held responsible that this order is observed, and they will march habitually in the rear of their regiments—company commanders in the rear of their respective companies.

They will suffer no men of their command to fall behind them on any excuse, except by a written permit of the Medical Officer of the regiment, that they are too sick to perform the march, and therefore must ride in ambulances.

Medical officers will be responsible that no such written pass is improperly given.

Regimental trains will march in rear of the divisions to which the regiments belong in the order of precedence of the regiments in that division. Brigade and division supply trains will follow in the rear of the respective army corps to which they belong.

Ambulance and ammunition wagons will follow in rear of their respective regiments, and under no consideration whatever, will any wagon or other vehicle be placed in the column of march, other than as hereinbefore specified.

Officers and soldiers of this army will habitually carry two days' cooked rations upon their persons when ordered to perform a march.

It is recommended to commanders of Corps d'armee that in all cases when it is practicable, the shelter tents and knapsacks of the men be carried in the wagons.

At least one hundred rounds of ammunition per man will be carried habitually in the cartridge-boxes and on the persons of the men, and any Captain of a company, whose men at any time are defficient in this amount of ammunition, will be arrested and reported to the War Department for dismissal from the service. A proper staff officer will be sent from these Headquarters to inspect the troops while on the march, who will report to the Major-General commanding, any violation of, or departure from the provisions of this order. Neither officer nor soldier will be permitted to leave his command while on the march, or enter any house, without a written permit from his Brigade commander. Where soldiers are obliged for necessary purposes to leave the ranks while on the march, they will turn over their muskets and accoutrements to the next men on their right, who will carry the arms accoutrements, and be responsible for them till the owners shall have again taken their places in the ranks.

Commanders of Corps will prescribe the number of rounds of artillery ammunition to be carried with each battery; but in no case shall any battery be left with less than 200 rounds for each gun. As good order and decipline are essential to the success of any army, a strict compliance with the provisions of this order is enjoined upon all officers and soldiers of this command, and they are expected and required to report to their superior officers every departure from them. While the Major-General commanding the army will see to it that every soldier is kindly cared for, and supplied with everything necessary for his comfort, he takes occasion to announce to the army, that the severest punishment will be inflicted upon every officer and soldier who neglects his duty, and connives at, or conceals any such neglect of duty or disobedience of orders on the part of any other officer or soldier.

Commanders of Army Corps will see that this order is published immediately after the receipt at the head of every regiment in their command.

By command of Maj.-Gen. Pope.

R. O. Selfridge, Asst. Adjt.-Gen.

Official: T. C. H. Smith, Lieut.-Col., and A. D. C.

	Infty.	Arty.	Cav.	Total.
First Army Corps,........	10,550	948	1,730	13,228
Second Army Corps,..............13,343		1,224	4,104	18,671
Third Army Corps,..............17,604		971	2,904	21,479
Total,.................... 41,497		3,143	8,738	53,378

Deduct Int'ty Brig. stationed at Winchester,...........2,500
Deduct Regiment and Battery at Front Royal, ...1,000
Deduct Cavalry unfit for service, ...3,000   6,500
Total,...46,878

(See correspondence on the subject with Gen. Banks.)

NOTE—Instead of 14,500 infantry and artillery Banks had only about 8,000, from his report to me after the battle of Cedar Mountains.

I certify that this is a true copy of the consolidated morning report of the Army of Virginia, dated July 31st, 1862, commanded by Maj. Gen. Pope.

Myer Asch, Capt. and A. D. C.

UNITED STATES MILITARY TELEGRAPH,
War Department, Washington, D. C., June 30th, 1862.
Middletown, June 30th,—1.10 p. m.

Time received: 1-45 p. m.

(Extract.)

Maj.-Gen. John Pope: *   *   *   The troops forming 1st Corps are not in good condition. They are weakened and poorly provided. The organization is not complete, and the whole cavalry force consists of not more than eight hundred (800) effective men and horses. They are scarcely sufficient for picket and patrol duty, so that I can hardly make a reconnoissance.   *   *   *   *

(Signed)   F. Sigel, Maj.-Gen. Commanding.

A true copy: T. C. H. Smith, Lt.-Col., and A. D. C.

Dispatches and orders sent and received from Aug. 8, to Aug. 20, inclusive.

HEADQUARTERS ARMY OF VIRGINIA,
Culpepper C. H., Aug. 8, 1862.

Major Gen. Halleck, Washington,—One Division of the enemy, Elzey's, crossed the Rapidan to-day, at Barnett's Ford, about five miles west of the railroad crossing, and rested at Robertson's River.

This is probably a reconnoissance in force, but it may be possibly an advance upon Culpepper. One Division of McDowell's and the whole of Banks' Corps are here to-night. Sigel's will be here to-morrow morning, when I will push the enemy again behind the Rapidan, and take up a strong position as you suggest in your dispatch of this date. I will be very careful that my communications with Fredericksburg are not interrupted. We captured to-day about forty prisoners from the enemy, our loss being one cavalry soldier killed, and one wounded.

I have directed King to march to-morrow and cross the Rapidan on the plank road at Germania Mills, or Ely's Ford, just below it. It is about 35 miles from Fredericksburg to this point.

(Signed)   Jno. Pope, Maj.-Gen., Commanding.

A true copy: T. C. H. Smith, Liut.-Col. and A. D. C.

HEADQUARTERS, ARMY OF VIRGINIA, }
Culpepper, C. H., Aug. 8, 1862. }

General:—The General commanding directs me, in reply to your dispatch of this date, 6:50 P. M., inquiring what road you shall take, to say that you are to march direct to Culpepper C. H., by the turnpike. He is surprised that you make this inquiry after his definite instructions of this morning. He directs that you reach this point by 12 M. to-morrow.

With great respect, General, your obd't serv't,

[Signed]   T. C. H. Smith, Lieut.-Col. and A. D. C.

Maj.-Gen. Sigel, Com. 1st Army Corps.

A true copy: T. C. H. Smith, Lieut.-Col. and A. D. C.

Received at Headquarters 2d Army Corps, 8:40 A. M. 9th August.

MADISON COURT-HOUSE, Aug. 8.

To Maj.-Gen. Banks:—All of my force is withdrawn from Madison Court-House, and is in retreat toward Sperryville. The enemy is in force on both my right and left, and in my rear. I may be cut off.

[Signed]   John Buford, Brigadier-General.

Received by signal, 8 a. m., Fairfax, Va.

A true copy: T. C. H. Smith, Lieut-Col. and A. D. C.

HEADQUARTERS, 3D ARMY CORPS, ARMY OF VIRGINIA, }
Culpepper Court-House, August 9, 1862. }

Maj.-Gen. Pope, &c.—*General:* I have just received a letter from the Colonel of the Rhode Island cavalry, who says: "All is quiet in front of us. The enemy is always before my videttes; on my left there is, perhaps, a regiment of rebel infantry. In a word, I do not believe the enemy to be in force in our front. Gen. Bayard has just ordered me to march to repulse the enemy."

Very, respectfully, General, your obedient servant,

[Signed]   Irwin McDowell,

Major-General, Commanding, 3d A. C. A. V.

A true copy: T. C. H. Smith, Lieut.-Col. and A. D. C.

HEADQUARTERS ARMY OF VIRGINIA, SECOND CORPS, }
Two hours, 25 min., 9th Aug., 1862. }

Major-Gen. Pope:—Gen. William's Division has taken position on
the Pike, the right on a heavy body of woods. Gen. Augur on the left,
his left resting on a mountain, occupied by his skirmishers. He will
soon be in position. The enemy shows his cavalry (which is strong)
ostentatiously. No infantry seen, and not much artillery. Woods on
left said to be full of troops. A visit to the front does not impress
that the enemy intends immediate attack. He seems, however, to be
taking positions.
[Signed] N. P. Banks.
A true copy: T. C. H. Smith, Lieut.-Col. and A. D. C.

———

HEADQUARTERS ARMY SECOND CORPS, }
4 hours 50 min., Aug. 9, 1862. }

Col. Ruggles, Chief of Staff:—About 4 o'clock shots were ex-
changed by the skirmishers. Artillery opened fire on both sides in
a few minutes. One regiment of rebel infantry advancing, now deploying in front as skirmishers. I have ordered a regiment on the
right, William's Division, to meet them, and one from the left,
Auger's, to advance on the left and in front.
5 p. m. [Signed] N. P. Banks.
They are now approaching each other.
A true copy: T. C. H. Smith, Lieut.-Col. and A. D. C.

———

UNITED STATES MILITARY TELEGRAPH, }
From War Department, Washington, Aug. 18, 1862. }

To Gen. Pope:—I fully approve your movement. I hope to push
a part of Burnside's forces to near Barnett's Ford by to-morrow
night, to assist you in holding that pass. Stand firm on the line of
the Rappahannock till I can help you. Fight hard and aid will soon
come. H. W. Halleck, Gen.-in-Chief.
A true copy; T. C. H. Smith, Lieut.-Col. and A. D. C.

———

HEADQUARTERS ARMY OF VIRGINIA, }
Rappahannock Station, August 20, 1862. }

Major-Gen. Halleck: Your dispatch of yesterday, received last
night. I shall mass my whole force along what is known as Marsh
Run, about two and a half or three miles north-east of Rappahannock
Ford, occupying Kelly's Ford with an advanced guard from my left,
Rappahannock Ford with an advanced guard from the center, and
picketing strongly with cavalry the fords above me as far as the
road from Sperryville to Warrenton. If the enemy attempt to turn
my right by the way of Sulphur Springs, they will probably march
direct on Warrenton, from which place a good turnpike conducts to
Washington. Such a movement, however, will expose their flank and
rear, and you may be sure I will not lose the opportunity. My right
will be considerably refused along the railroad as far at least as Bealton Station. What relations with me will the Corps of Fitz John

Porter have? I should like to know exactly. I am going out to post my command. I have heard from Reno. He crossed safely yesterday at Kelly's Ford and Barnett's Ford. The enemy so far has made no movement in advance. I think they are not yet ready, for want of transportation for supplies, to cross the Rapidan.

John Pope, Maj.-Gen.

A true copy: T. C. H. Smith, Lt.-Col. and A. D. C.

Dispatches and Orders sent and received from Aug. 21st to 24th, inclusive.

UNITED STATES MILITARY TELEGRAPH, }
Received Aug. 21st, 1862, from War Department, Washington. }

To General Pope:—I have telegraphed Gen. Burnside to know at what hour he can re-enforce Reno. Am waiting his answer. Every effort must be made to hold the Rappahannock. Large forces will be in to-morrow.

(Signed) H. W. Halleck, General in Chief.

A true copy: T. C. H. Smith, Liut.-Col. and A. D. C.

HEADQUARTERS ARMY OF VIRGINIA, }
Rappahannock Station, Aug. 21st, 1862. }

Maj.-Gen. Halleck:—The enemy has made no further advance since yesterday afternoon, but his cavalry pickets are in plain view of our front. After full examination of the ground I have determined to maintain the line of the Rappahannock instead of Marsh Creek. I have accordingly occupied advanced and commanding positions on the south side of the river, and have three bridges besides the fords, to connect with them. The main body of my command is posted along the north side of the river, having easy access to the front. I have masked the fords above and below me with infantry, cavalry and artillery, and have no concern about any attack in the front, though as previously suggested, my right can be turned at considerable distance above me. This, however, will require time, and will be, besides, a hazardous operation. We drew back behind the Rappahannock in perfect order, without leaving any article whatever.

(Signed) John Pope, Major-General.

A true copy: T. C. H. Smith, Lieut.-Col. and A. D. C.

UNITED STATES MILITARY TELEGRAPH, }
War Department Washington, August 21st, 1862. }

To General Pope:—I have have just sent Gen. Burnside's reply. Gen. Cox's forces are coming in from Parkersburg, and will be here to-morrow and the next day. Dispute every inch of ground, and fight like the devil, till we can reinforce you. Forty-eight hours more, and we can make you strong enough. Don't yield an inch if you can help it.

H. W. Halleck, General-in-Chief.

A true copy: T. C. H. Smith, Lieut.-Col. and A. D. C.

HEADQUARTERS, ARMY OF VIRGINIA, }
Rappahannock Station, Aug. 22d, 1862—12 o'clock m. }
· *Commanding Officer, Warrenton Junction:*—Keep your cavalry scouring the roads and pick up stragglers. You will keep them under guard at Catlett's Station, or use them for fatigue duty.
By order of Maj.-Gen. Pope.
(Signed) Geo. D. Ruggles, Col. and Chief of Staff.
A true copy: T. C. H. Smith, Lieut.-Col. and A. D. C.

HEADQUARTERS, ARMY OF VIRGINIA, }
Rappahannock Station, Aug. 22d, 1862—12 o'clock, m. }
Major-General Halleck:—The number of stragglers leaving this army just now, and the ease with which they escape, are becoming serious. Can they not be arrested and confined in prison at Washington, as I have not at present the means to bring them here, or to keep them when I get them?
(Singed) John Pope, M. G.
A true copy: T. C. H. Smith, Lieut.-Col. and A. D. C.

HEADQUARTERS, ARMY OF VIRGINIA, }
Aug. 22d, 1862—10-30 a. m. }
Major General Halleck:—It is very apparent that the enemy is moving, with a view of turning our right. He has no forces further east than Stevensburg, and everything is tending up the river. I presume he will cross, if possible, at Sulphur Springs, on the pike to Washington. I would suggest that all the forces being sent from Fredericksburg be pushed forward immediately as far as this place, as I think there is no danger whatever on the lower fords of the Rappahannock. A captured letter from Gen. Robert Lee to Gen. Stuart, dated at Gordonsville, Aug. 15, clearly indicates their movement. We had several handsome skirmishes yesterday, in one of which one of our cavalry regiments, on the south side of the river, charged over a regiment of rebel infantry, dispersing them and driving them into the woods. Seventy head of the enemy's beef cattle and seven horses were captured. There has been heavy artillery firing all this morning, the enemy not yet having finished his preparation for attack. My whole force is massed and well in hand. We have had a great many casualties within the last two days of skirmishing and cannonading. I cannot tell how many.
(Signed) John Pope, Maj.-Gen.
A true copy: T. C. H. Smith, Lt.-Col. and A. D. C.

HEADQUARTERS, Army of VIRGINIA, }
Rappahannock Station, Aug. 22d, 5 o'clock p. m., 1862. }
Major General Halleck:—I think that the troops of Heintzelman and Cox had best be landed from the train at Bealton Station, Kearney on or near Licking River, say two miles south-west of Warrentown Junction. The enemy has made no attempt to-day to cross the river. His movement up toward our right seems to have been con-

tinued all day. I have little doubt if he crosses at all, it will be at Sulphur Springs. Under present circumstances I shall not attempt to prevent his crossing at Sulphur Springs, but will mass my whole force on his flank in the neighborhood of Fayetteville. By undertaking to defend the crossing at Sulphur Springs I would much extend my lines and remove myself too far from the reenforcements that are arriving by railroad. Before the enemy can be fairly across the river with any considerable force, I shall be strong enough to advance from Fayetteville upon his flank.

(Signed)   John Pope, Major-General.
A true copy: T. C. H. Smith, Lieut.-Col. and A. D. C.

HEADQUARTERS ARMY OF VIRGINIA, }
Rappahannock Station, Aug 22d—6.30 oclock, p. m. }

Major-General Halleck:— Every thing indicates clearly to me that the enemy's movement will be upon Warrenton by way of Sulphur Springs. If I could know with anything like certainty by what time to expect troops that are starting from Alexandria, I could act more understandingly. I have not heard of the arrival of any of the forces from Fredericksburg at the fords below, though I have withdrawn nearly the whole of Reno's forces from Kelly's ford. I cannot move against Sulphur Springs just now without exposing my rear to the heavy force in front of me, and having my communication with the forces coming up the Rappahannock intercepted, and most likely the railroad destroyed. I think it altogether well to bring Franklin's force to Alexandria. Lee made his headquarters at Culpepper last night. He has the whole of his army in front of me. Its numbers you can estimate as well as myself. As soon as his plans are fully developed I shall be ready to act.

(Signed)   John Pope, Major-General.
Official: T. C. H. Smith, Lt.-Col. and A. D. C.

HEADQUARTERS ARMY OF VIRGINIA, }
Rappahannock Station, Aug. 22d, 1862—9 p. m. }

Major-General Halleck:—Scouts report a heavy force moving up across Hedgeman River, on the Sperryville and Little Washington Pike, toward Warrenton; also crossing at Sulphur Springs. I think a Brigade should be sent to guard the railroad bridge at Cedar Run, and that Heintzelman's Corps should be hurried forward with all possible dispatch.

(Signed)   John Pope, Major-General.
A true copy: T. C. H. Smith, Lieut.-Col. and A. D. C.

HEADQUARTERS, ARMY OF VIRGINIA, }
Aug. 22d—9.15 p. m. }

Gen. Halleck:—Reports from our forces near Sulphur Springs just in. Enemy was crossing river to day at Sulphur Springs, and on the road from Warrenton to Sperryville; he is still in heavy force at Rappahannock ford, and above, and my rear is entirely exposed, if I move toward Sulphur Springs or Warrenton. I must do one of two things : either fall back and meet Heintzelman behind Cedar Run, or cross the Rappahannock, with my whole force and assail the enemy's flank and rear. I must do one or the other at daylight. Which shall it be? I incline to the latter, but don't wish to interfere with your plans.

(Signed)   John Pope, Major-General.
A true copy: T. C. H. Smith, Lt.-Col., and A. D. C.

UNITED STATES MILITARY TELEGRAPH,
Received Aug. 22d, 1862, from War Department,
Washington, August 22d, 1862—11 p. m.

To Major-General Pope :—I think the latter of your two propositions the best. I also think you had better stop Heintzelman's Corps, and the troops of Sturgis and Cox, as they arrive to-morrow at Warrenton Junction, instead of taking them to Bealton.

(Signed)   H. W. Halleck, General-in-Chief.
A true copy: T. C. H. Smith, Lieut.-Col. and A. D. C.

UNITED STATES MILITARY TELEGRAPH,
Received Aug. 22, 1862. From Manasses 10·04 p. m.

To General Pope :—We will continue to forward troops to Manassas unless you order otherwise; but beyond this point trains will be held to wait your orders, or until further information is received.

(Signed)   Haupt.
A true copy: T. C. H. Smith, Lieut.-Col., and A. D. C.

HEADQUARTERS ARMY OF VIRGINIA,
Rappahannock Station, Aug. 23, 1862—2·20 o'clock a. m.

Major General Halleck :—As nearly as I can learn the facts, the enemy's cavalry made a raid from the direction of Warrenton upon our wagon trains at Catlett's, and seems to have done some considerable damage to them through the gross carelessness of the guard, which was amply sufficient to protect them. Please hurry forward Heintzelman, as the enemy may reach Warrenton Junction before he does. Please push forward also, all the troops moving up from Fredericksburg, with orders to cross the Rappahannock at the various fords, and march rapidly on Stevensburg. My movement will be made to-morrow, as soon as I find the enemy has passed a sufficient number of his troops over the river. The troops coming up from Fredericksburg should be hastened forward with all dispatch to Stevensburg and Brandy Station. It will be well, also, to send with them immediately a train of bread, sugar, coffee and salt, as our railroad communications may be unsafe for a few days.

(Signed)   John Pope, Major-General.
A true copy: T. C. H. Smith, Lieut.-Col. and A. D. C.

HEADQUARTERS 1ST CORPS ARMY OF VA.,
Aug. 23d, 1862.

Major General Pope, Commanding Army of Va. :—There is no

doubt that the enemy has outflanked us, and that his army crosses near Sulphur Springs and Fox's or Lawson's Ford. I therefore must instantly beg you to send Gen. Reno's Division to Fayetteville, which will be good and necessary for all emergencies—but it should be done to-night, and immediately. Gen. Banks, instead of marching to Lawson's Ford, as directed by me, has not done it, and the enemy is therefore crossing at Fox's Ford, from which ford Gen. Bayard retired an hour ago. From Fayetteville Gen. Reno can advance to Lawson's Ford, or maintain his position until you have made your proper arrangements. It would be, according to my opinion, the best to withdraw the 1st Corps toward Bealton, or my original position near Beverly Ford, to enable us to concentrate all our forces in a central position. Gen Reno would cover this movement, and we would gain one day. I am, General, respectfully yours

(Signed) F. Sigel, Major-Gen. Com'ding 1st Corps.

A true copy: T. C. H. Smith, Lieut.-Col. and A. D. C.

HEADQUARTERS ARMY OF VIRGINIA, }
August 23, 1862. }

Major-Gen. Sigel:—Your dispatch just received. Gen. Buford is at Fayetteville, and will watch any movement of the enemy toward that place, or toward your right. Stand firm and let the enemy develop toward Warrenton. Re-inforcements are constantly arriving in our rear. I do not wish any further extension of our lines to the right, but I desire the enemy to cross as large a force as he pleases in the direction of Warrenton. When I wish to concentrate on the railroad I will cover your movement back. Be under no concern, but keep your whole command ready to march at a moment's notice. Send word to Bayard to keep his position as far up the river as possible, and check, if you find it necessary, any attempt of the enemy to cross at Lawson's Ford.

By order of Gen. Pope.

[Signed] T. C. H. Smith, Lt.-Col. and A. D. C.

A true copy : T. C. H. Smith, Lt.-Col. and A. D. C.

HEADQUARTERS ARMY OF VIRGINIA, }
Aug. 23, 1862—7:15 o'clock a. m. }

Major-Gen. Sigel:—The river has risen here six feet, and is entirely impassable at any ford. I have no doubt it is the same all the way up the river, as the main portion of the storm was above. The enemy, therefore, on this side is cut off from those on the other, and there is no fear of this' position. You will accordingly march at once upon Sulphur Springs, and thence toward Waterloo Bridge, attacking and beating the enemy wherever you find them. Banks' Corps and the force under Gen. Reno will accompany and support you. McDowell, with his whole Corps, marches direct on Warrenton, and you will be brought together in that neighborhood to-night. Move promptly up the river. The other troops will be close behind you. You ought to be in the neighborhood of Waterloo Bridge before sunset. I will accompany McDowell's Corps, and communicate further with you in the course of the day. You will have an effective force of 25,000 men. Leave nothing behind you.

[Signed]   Jno. Pope, Major-Gen.
A true copy : T. C. H. Smith, Lt.-Col. and A. D. C.

HEADQUARTERS ARMY OF VIRGINIA, }
Aug. 23, 1862—7:35 o'clock, a. m. }

Maj.-Gen. Banks :—You will accompany and support Gen. Sigel in his forward movements toward Sulphur Springs and Waterloo Bridge. Gen. Reno will follow you closely for the same purpose. McDowell's Corps marches immediately upon Warrenton. The river has risen six feet, and is no longer passable by the enemy. His forces on this side are cut off from those on the other, and we will march against those on this side, and the whole force will unite between Warrenton and Waterloo Bridge. Call in Crawford at once, and leave nothing behind you. Follow Sigel very closely, and keep constant communication with him, as also with Gen. Reno in your rear. Be quick, for time is everything.

[Signed]   Jno. Pope, Maj.-Gen.
A true copy: T. C. H. Smith, Lt.-Col. and A. D. C.

HEADQUARTERS ARMY OF VIRGINIA, }
Rappahannock Station, Aug. 23, 1862—9 a. m. }

Maj.-Gen. Halleck :—The heavy storm of yesterday and last night has caused the river to rise six feet. There are no longer any fords, and the bridges are carried away. I succeeded in time in withdrawing my advanced forces from the south side of the river. The movement across the river on the enemy's flank and rear is therefore impossible. The enemy's forces on this side, which have crossed at Sulphur Springs and Hedgeman's River, are cut off from those on the south side. I march at once with my whole force on Sulphur Springs, Waterloo Bridge and Warrenton, in the hope to destroy these forces before the river runs down. The rain still continues, and I think we are good for thirty-six hours. As soon as I have effected this purpose, which I expect to do by an early hour to-morrow, I shall move back, detaching a large force to re-open my communications at Catlett's and send forward supplies. If Heintzelman and Cox move quickly it will be easy to hold the Rappahannock, leaving the enemy much damaged by his attempt to turn our right. You may not hear from me before to-morrow night.

[Signed]   John Pope, Major-General.
A true copy : T. C. H. Smith, Lieut.-Col. and A. D. C.

HEADQUARTERS ARMY OF VIRGINIA, }
August 23, 1862—11 o'clock a. m. }

Gen. Reynolds :—You will please on arriving at Rappahannock Station, follow the route taken by the Army Corps of Gen. McDowell, passing Brig.-Gen. Tower who is in command of the rear guard, and

whom you will find near the railroad station. Please keep well closed and close up to the rear of McDowell's Corps. Our march is to Warrenton, about ten miles distant, which you must make to-night.
By order of Major-Gen. Pope, Commanding Army of Virginia.
[Signed]   T. C. H. Smith, Lieut.-Col. and A. D. C.
A true copy: T. C. H. Smith, Lieut. Col. and A. D. C.

HEADQUARTERS ARMY OF VIRGINIA, }
Near Warrenton, August 23, 1862—10 o'clock p. m. }
Major-Gen. Halleck:—My advance entered the town about an hour ago, the enemy evacuating it on our approach. They fell back toward Hedgeman's River and Sulphur Springs. At the latter place my left was engaged about sunset, and now awaits daylight. I shall move rapidly at daylight upon Sulphur Springs and Waterloo Bridge. If the enemy is really in large force on this side of the Rappahannock, he will be trapped, as the river is very high behind him. I will communicate to-morrow.
[Signed]   Jno. Pope, Major-General.
A true copy: T. C. H. Smith, Lieut.-Col. and A. D. C.

HEADQUARTERS ARMY OF VIRGINIA, }
Aug. 24, 1862—5 o'clock a. m. }
Major-Gen. Sigel, Commanding, &c.:—The advance Division of McDowell's Corps occupied Warrenton last night without opposition. The head of his column was pushed just outside of town, on the road to Sulphur Springs, ready to move forward to that point should it be necessary. I am pushing a reconnoissance toward Waterloo Bridge to see what is there. Communicate fully to me through Capt. Merrill, who will hand you this note, the condition of things in front of you. Our work must be finished here to-day. We have no time to spare. Provisions will be in Warrenton this morning.
[Signed]   Jno. Pope, Major-General.
A true copy: T. C. H. Smith, Lt.-Col. and A. D. C.

UNITED STATES MILITARY TELEGRAPH, }
Received Aug. 24, 1862, from Alexandria, Aug. 24, 1862. }
[Extract.]
To Maj.-Gen. Pope:— * * * Thirty thousand (30,000) troops or more demand transportation. It is clear that the sudden demand exceeds the capacity of the road. We can manage twelve thousand (12,000) troops per day, with supplies, if no accident occurs. The new troops might march; the veterans go in cars; horses driven. Baggage, tents, &c., wait until they can be forwarded; supplies take precedence.   [Signed]   Haupt.

UNITED STATES MILITARY TELEGRAPH,
Alexandria, Aug. 24, 1862.
[Extract.]

Major-Gen. Pope:—   *   *   *   *   We expect to clean out all the troops now here, and all that are expected to-day.   *
*   *   *   *

[Signed]   H. Haupt.

HEADQUARTERS FIRST CORPS, NEAR WATERLOO BRIDGE,
August 25, 1862—1:10 p. m.

Col. Geo. D. Ruggles, Chief of Staff:—Col. Beardsley reports the enemy's cavalry at Sulphur Springs, and the village occupied by the enemy's infantry. Col. Beardsley had been sent by me to Sulphur Springs, with some cavalry and mountain howitzers. The main force of the enemy is advancing on this place (Waterloo Bridge) Gen. Reno should send me the 20 pound Parrotts. I could use them here excellently. I am, Colonel, very respectfully,

[Signed]   F. Sigel, Major-Gen. Commanding 1st Corps.
A true copy: T. C. H. Smith, Lt. Col. and A. D. C.

HEADQUARTERS ARMY OF VIRGINIA,
Warrenton, Aug. 24, 1862—3:45 p. m.

Major-Gen. Halleck, General-in-Chief, Washington: I arrived in Warrenton last night; the enemy had left two hours previously. Milroy's Brigade, the advance of Sigel's Corps, came upon the enemy late yesterday afternoon, near Great Run, about four miles from Warrenton Sulphur Springs, and near the mouth of it. A sharp action took place which lasted till after dark, the enemy being driven across Great River, but destroying the bridge behind him. Early this morning Gen. Buford reached Waterloo Bridge, which was defended by a considerable force of the enemy and one piece of artillery. He took possession of the bridge and destroyed it.

Sigel's force advanced again on the left this morning, and when last heard from was pursuing the enemy in the direction of Waterloo Bridge. His column was being shelled from the opposite bank of the river, which is still too deep to be forded. The enemy has made no advance against Rappahannock Station since we left, though yesterday morning while we were withdrawing our forces from the opposite side of the river, he brought forward his columns of infantry and attempted to carry the heights we were leaving by storm. He was, however, repulsed with considerable loss. We have had a continuous engagement, principally with artillery, along the whole line of the river for eight or ten miles, during the last three days.

No force of the enemy has yet been able to cross except that now enclosed by our forces between Sulphur Springs and Waterloo Bridge, which will no doubt be captured, unless they find some means, of which I know nothing, of escaping across the river between those places.

Early to-morrow, after clearing this side of the river, I shall move back a considerable part of this force to the neighborhood of Rappahannock Station. By that time the river will doubtless be fordable again. I shall leave a corps of observation here to watch the crossings at Waterloo and Sulphur Springs. The forces arriving from Washington and Alexandria will be assembled, I think, on Licking River, between Germantown and the railroad, with a reserve for the force at Warrenton, somewhere between Warrenton Junction and this place—until you are ready to begin a forward movement.

I cannot form an estimate of the forces of the enemy. He has been developed in heavy force, by simultaneous reconnoissances, along a line of nine miles from the railroad crossing of the Rappahannock, as far, at least, as Sulphur Springs. I should like to have some idea of the forces which are coming here, and your plans of organizing them, that they may be assigned and posted in some order.

Our losses during the last three days have been quite heavy, among the killed being Brig.-Gen. Bohlen, commanding a brigade in Sigel's Corps. The whole tendency of the enemy since he appeared in front of us at Rappahannock Station, has been toward our right, but how far his movement in that direction will extend, I am not able to say. I shall to-morrow remove my headquarters to some central point, probably Warrenton Junction.

John Pope, Major-General Commanding.
A true copy: T. C. H. Smith, Lieut.-Col. and A. D. C.

HEADQUARTERS ARMY OF VIRGINIA, }
Warrenton, Aug. 24th, 1862. }

General:—To-night or at an early hour in the morning, you will please send spies and scouts around by Front Royal to Thornton's Gap, and into the Valley of the Shenandoah, to ascertain whether any of the enemy's forces are moving in that direction. Send at least two or three reliable men for that purpose, and instruct them that if they find any difficulty in returning to you they shall go into Winchester, and communicate their information to Gen. White. You will receive instructions as to your movements in the morning.

By order of Gen. Pope.
T. C. H. Smith, Lieut.-Col. and A. D. C.

Major-Gen. Sigel, Commanding. &c.
A true copy: T. C. H. Smith, Lieut.-Col. and A. D. C.

HEADQUARTERS FIRST CORPS ARMY OF VIRGINIA, }
Near Waterloo Bridge, Va., Aug. 24th, 1862. }

Col. Geo. D. Ruggles, Chief of Staff Army of Virginia:—The First Corps is in bivouac at Waterloo Bridge, with the exception of an infantry brigade left at Sulphur Springs, as rear guard, together with a brigade of Gen. Banks, and one of Gen. Reno.

Gen. Banks' Corps is on the Sulphur Springs road, about four miles from the Springs, and Gen. Reno is at or near the fork of the Warrenton road.

To judge from the appearance of the camp fires and camps, I am certain that the enemy's main army is encamped on the other side of the river, perhaps two miles from the river, with the advance at Amissville, and the rear opposite Sulphur Springs.

(Signed)   F. Sigel, Maj.-Gen. Commanding First Corps.
A true copy : T. C. H. Smith, Lt.-Col. and A. D. C.

Dispatches and Orders sent and Received from Aug. 25th, to Aug. 28th, inclusive.

HEADQUARTERS ARMY OF VIRGINIA, {
August 25th, 1862. {

Major-General Halleck :—Your dispatch just received. Of course I shall be ready to re-cross the Rappahannock at a moment's notice. You will see from the positions taken that each army Corps is on the best roads across the river. You wished forty-eight hours to assemble the forces from the Peninsula behind the Rappahannock, and four days have passed without the enemy yet being permitted to cross. I don't think he is ready yet to do so. In ordinary dry weather the Rappahannock can be crossed almost anywhere, and these crossing places are best protected by concentrating at central positions to strike at any force which attempts to cross. I had clearly understood that you wished to unite our whole forces before a forward movement was begun, and that I must take care to keep united with Burnside on my left, so that no movement to separate us could be made. This withdrew me lower down the Rappahannock than I wished to come. I am not acquainted with your views, as you seem to suppose, and would be glad to know them as far as my own position and operations are concerned. I understood you clearly that at all hazards I was to prevent the enemy from passing the Rappahannock. This I have done and shall do. I don't like to be on the defensive if I can help it, but must be so as long as I am tied to Burnside's forces, not yet wholly arrived at Fredericksburg. Please let me know, if it can be done, what is to be my own command, and if I am to act independently against the enemy. I certainly understood that, as soon as the whole of our forces were concentrated, you designed to take command in person, and that, when every thing was ready, we were to move forward in concert. I judge from the tone of your dispatch that you are dissatisfied with something. Unless I know what it is, of course, I can't correct it. The troops arriving here come in fragments. Am I to assign them to Brigades and Corps? I would suppose not, as several of the new regiments coming have been assigned to Army Corps directly from your office. In case I commence offensive operations I must know what forces I am to take, and what you wish left, and what connection must be kept up with Burnside. It has been my purpose to conform my operations to your plans. yet I was not informed when McClellan evacuated Harrison's, so that I might know what to expect in that direction ; and when I say these things, in no complaining spirit, I think you know well that I am anxious to do everything to advance your plans of campaign. I understood that this Army was to maintain the line of the Rappahannock until all the forces from the

Peninsula had united behind that river. I have done so. I understood distinctly that I was not to hazard anything except for this purpose, as delay was what was wanted.

The enemy this morning has pushed a considerable infantry force up opposite Waterloo Bridge, and is planting batteries, and long lines of his infantry are moving up from Jeffersonville towards Sulphur Springs. His whole force, as far as can be ascertained, is massed in front of me, from railroad crossing of Rappahannock around to Waterloo Bridge, their main body being opposite Sulphur Springs.

(Signed)   John Pope, Major-General.

A true copy : T. C. H. Smith, Lieut.-Col., and A. D. C.

[Extract.]

UNITED STATES MILITARY TELEGRAPH,   }
Received Aug. 26, 1862—from War Department 11:45 a. m. }

To Maj.-Gen. Pope :—Not the slightest dissatisfaction has been felt in regard to your operations on the Rappahannock. The main object has been accomplished in getting up troops from the Peninsula, although they have been delayed by storms. Moreover, the telegraph has been interrupted, leaving us for a time ignorant of the progress of the evacuation.   *   *   *   *   *   *

(Signed.)   H. W. Halleck, Gen.-in-Chief.

A true copy: T. C. H. Smith, Lieut.-Col. and A. D. C.

HEADQUARTERS THIRD CORPS, }
Aug. 25—11:25 a. m. }

Col. Ruggles, A. A. G. and Chief of Staff—Colonel:—Inclosed you will please find reports of Col. Clark, A. D. C., from the Signal Corps Station, of the movements of the enemy on the south side of Hedgeman or Rappahannock River. The facts are reported as having been observed by himself, and can be relied upon as being as near the truth as the distance will permit. It seems to be apparent that the enemy is threatening, or moving upon the Valley of the Shenandoah via Front Royal, with designs upon the Potomac—possibly beyond. Not knowing whether you have received this information, I forward it for the consideration of the Commanding General.

Respectfully, &c.,   N. P. Banks, M.-G. C.

A true copy: T. C. H. Smith, Lieut.-Col. and A. D. C.

WARRENTON JUNCTION, }
August 25, 1862—9.30 p. m. }

Maj. Gen. Sigel, Commanding 1st Corps :—You will force the passage of the river at Waterloo Bridge to-morrow morning at day light, and see what is in front of you. I do not believe there is any enemy in force there, but do believe that the whole of their army has marched to the west and northwest.

I am not satisfied either with your reports or your operations of to-day, and expect to hear to-morrow early something more satisfactory concerning the enemy. Send back and bring up your provision trains to your command, but no regimental trains or baggage of any description. You will consider this a positive order, to be obeyed literally. You will communicate with me by telegraph from Warrenton.

John Pope, Major-General Commanding.
Sent in the care of Gen. McDowell, at Warrenton.
A true copy: T. C. H. Smith, Lt.-Col. and A. D. C.

WARRENTON JUNCTION,
Aug. 25, 1862—9:30 p. m.

Maj.-Gen. McDowell, Warrenton:—I believe that the whole force of the enemy has marched for the Shenandoah Valley, by way of Luray and Front Royal. The column which has marched to-day toward Gaines' Cross Roads has turned north, and when last seen was passing under the east base of Buck Mountain, toward Salem and Rectortown. I desire you, as early as possible in the morning, holding Reynolds in reserve at Warrenton or vicinity, to make a reconnoissance with your whole Corps, and ascertain what is beyond the river at Sulphur Springs.

There is no force of the enemy between here and Culpepper, or at Culpepper.

I send you a dispatch for Gen. Sigel, which please read and send to him immediately.

Communicate with me frequently by telegraph from Warrenton.

John Pope, Major-General Commanding.
A true copy: T. C. H. Smith, Lieut -Col. and A. D. C.

UNITED STATES MILITARY TELEGRAPH,
Received August 26, 1862,
From Headquarters Third Corps, 3:30 p. m., Warrenton.

To Maj.-Gen. Pope:—Gen. Sigel's bridge train has arrived. I think it may be useful. Gen. Milroy burned the bridge at Waterloo before he retired from that place last night, and Buford says the fords near Waterloo are bad. I have directed the available forces of Sigel's cavalry, with a section of his artillery, to report to Gen. Buford this afternoon on the Waterloo Road, with three day's cooked rations. I have directed Buford to march at dawn to-morrow toward Chester Gap, to ascertain what direction the enemy have taken on our right, whether to Rectortown or Front Royal, through Chester Gap. He will either take the Carter Church Road, up the left bank of Carter's Run, or the road direct from this place to Chester Gap, as inquiries to be made this p. m. shall determine. However persons may have differed as to the force at Waterloo, Sulphur Springs, or elsewhere, all agree in one thing—the movement of the enemy toward our right from Rappahannock to Waterloo. Battalions, trains, batteries, all have the same direction. The force of the enemy now seems to be above Sulphur Springs. Under these views, in addition to Sigel's Corps, now here, I beg to suggest that Hooker and Kearney be marched at once in this direction, instead of the direction of Rappahannock Station, for, whether we attack them, or they attack us, the contest must come off, it seems to me, as things now stand, above rather than below Sulphur Springs. If they could make a march this p. m. toward either Sulphur Springs or Waterloo Bridge, it would be a movement I think in the right direction. What is the enemy's purpose is not easy to discover. Some have thought he means to march around our right through Rectortown to Washington. Others think that he intends going down the Shenandoah, either through Thornton's or Chester Gap. Either of these operations seems to me too hazardous for him to undertake, with us in his rear and flank. Others that it was his object to throw his trains around into the Valley, to draw his supplies from that direction, and have his front looking to the east rather than to the north. It is also thought that while a portion of his force has marched up the immediate right bank of the Rappahannock, a larger portion has gone through Culpepper up the Sperryville road. No doubt these various suppositions may have occurred to you, but I have thought it not inappropriate to recapitulate them here with reference to the concentration of forces in this direction, which I have herein suggested. Cannonading at Sulphur Springs still continues about the same. I have ordered Buford to send you a regiment of cavalry. I can't get hold of Bayard.

[Signed.]   Irwin McDowell.

I have just received your telegrams of 2-20 and 3-15 p. m. I trust that Buford's reconnoissance to-morrow will obtain the information you desire concerning the movements of the enemy across the Sperryville Pike, in the direction of Gaines' Cross-roads and Salem. I also received from Gen. Banks' signal officer the account of this movement. With reference to your inquiries as to what has occurred to make the presence of Cox here desirable, I made the suggestion, first, because in the general order issued, he was ordered to join Sigel at Fayetteville. As Sigel was here, and, as I understood, Cox was arriving in the cars, I thought if it could be done, time would be gained by his being landed here rather than at Warrenton Junction.

(Signed)   Irwin McDowell, Maj.-Gen. Comd'g.
A true copy : T. C. H. Smith, Lieut.-Col. and A. D. C.

UNITED STATES MILITARY TELEGRAPH,
Rec'd Aug. 26, 1862. From near Waterloo Bridge, 3-45 p. m.

To General Pope:—Trains and troops still passing over the same route. A deserter just come in says, Longstreet's Corps, embracing Anderson's, Jones', Kemper's, Whitney's and Evans' Divisions, are located in the woods back of Waterloo Bridge; think Hill's Division at Jefferson, Jackson's Corps somewhere above Longstreet's. He appears truthful, and I credit his story. The entire district from Jefferson to Culpepper, Sperryville, and as far as Barber's, covered with smoke and lines of dust. The deserter reports the arrival last evening of the greater portion of Longstreet's Corps at its present position.

(Signed)   John S. Clark, Col. and A. D. C.
A true copy : T. C. H. Smith, Lieut.-Col. and A. D. C.

HEADQUARTERS THIRD CORPS,
Warrenton, Aug. 26th.—9 p. m.

Major General Pope :—An intelligent negro has just come in to Gen. Buford from White Plains, and reports the advance of the enemy's column at that place. He says he saw himself at that place to-day, at 12 o'clock, two batteries of artillery, two regiments of cavalry, four regiments of infantry, and that they were moving in the direction of Thoroughfare Gap. The man's story is evidently to be relied upon. Gen. Buford says his statements are confirmed by his scouts, who report large trains passing up through Orleans to White Plains.

(Signed) Irwin McDowell, Major-Gen.

True copy : John Pope, Major General.

WARRENTON JUNCTION,
Aug. 26th, 1862—8 p. m.

Major General McDowell, Warrenton :—Fitz John Porter, with Sykes' and Morell's Divisions, will be within two miles and a half of Warrenton, on the Fayetteville road, to-morrow night. See if you cannot have the cross-roads repaired so that he can get from his position into the Sulphur Springs road with his artillery, if he should be needed. Will use all efforts to have Sturgis and Cox within three miles of you to-morrow night, and have requested Gen. Halleck to push forward Franklin at once, carrying his baggage and supplies by railroad to the point where the Manassas Gap railroad intersects the Warrenton Turnpike.

From that position he can either advance to your support or prevent your right from being turned from the direction of the Manassas Gap Railroad. I think our fight should be made at Warrenton, and if you can postpone it for two days everything will be right.

John Pope, Major-General Commanding.

A true copy : T. C. H. Smith, Lieut.-Col. and A. D. C.

HEADQUARTERS ARMY OF VIRGINIA,
Warrenton Junction. Aug 26th, 1862—3:20 p. m.

Maj.-Gen. Heintzelman, Commanding, &c. :—The Major General commanding the Army of Virginia directs me to send you the inclosed communication, and to request that you put a regiment on a train of cars, and send it down immediately to Manassas, to ascertain what has occurred, repair the telegraph wires, and protect the railroad there till further orders.

With great respect, General, your obedient servant,

(Signed) T. C. H. Smith, Lieut.-Col. and A. D. C.

A true copy : T. C. H. Smith. Lieut.-Col. and A. D. C.

HEADQUARTERS ARMY OF VIRGINIA,
August 26, 1862—12 p. m.

Gen McDowell : — Gen. Sigel reports the enemy's rear guard at Orleans to-night, with his main force encamped at White Plains. You will please ascertain very early in the morning whether this is so, and have the whole of your command in readiness to march. You had best ascertain it to-night, if you possibly can. Our communications have been interrupted by the enemy's cavalry, near Manassas. Whether his whole force, or the larger part of it, has gone round, is a question which we must settle instantly. And no portion of his force must march opposite to us, to-night, without our knowing it. I telegraphed you an hour or two ago, what dispositions I had made, supposing the advance through Thoroughfare to be a column of not more than ten or fifteen thousand men. If his whole force, or the larger part of it, has gone, we must know it at once. The troops here have no artillery, and if the main forces of the enemy are still opposite to you, you must send forward to Greenwich to be there to-morrow evening with two batteries of artillery, or three if you can get them, to meet Kearney. We must know at a very early hour in the morning, so as to determine our plans.

(Signed)   John Pope, Major-General.
A true copy: T. C. H. Smith, Lieut.-Col. and A. D. C.

HEADQUARTERS ARMY OF VIRGINIA, }
Warrenton Junction, August 27, 1862. }

General Orders No. –.—The following movement of troops will be made, viz:

Major-Gen. McDowell with his own and Sigel's Corps, and the Divisions of Brig.-Gen. Reynolds, will pursue the turnpike from Warrenton to Gainesville, if possible, to-night.

The Army Corps of Gen. Heintzelman, with the detachment of the Ninth Corps under Maj.-Gen. Reno leading, will take the road from Catlett's Station to Greenwich, so as to reach there to-night or early in the morning. Maj.-Gen. Reno will immediately communicate with Maj.-Gen. McDowell, and his command as well as that of Maj.-Gen. Heintzelman, will support Maj.-Gen. McDowell in any operations against the enemy.

Maj.-Gen. Fitz John Porter will remain at Warrenton Junction till he is relieved by Maj.-Gen. Banks, when he will immediately push forward with his Corps in the direction of Greenwich and Gainesville, to assist the operations on the right wing.

Major-Gen. Banks, as soon as he arrives at Warrenton Junction, will assume the charge of the trains, and cover their movement toward Manassas Junction. The train of his own corps, under escort of two regiments of infantry and a battery of artillery, will pursue the road south of the railroad, which conducts into the rear of Manassas Junction. As soon as all the trains have passed Warrenton Junction, he will take post behind Cedar Run, covering the fords and bridges of that stream, and holding his position as long as possible. He will cause all the railroad trains to be loaded with the public and private stores now here, and run them back toward Manassas Junction as far as the railroad is practicable. Wherever a bridge is burned, so as to prevent the further passage of the railroad trains, he will assemble them all as near together as possible, and protect them with his command until the bridges are rebuilt. If the enemy is too strong before him, before the bridge is repaired, he will be careful to destroy entirely the trains, locomotives, and stores before he falls back in the direction of Manassas Junction. He is, however, to understand that he is to defend his position as long as possible, keeping himself in constant communication with Major Gen. Porter on his right. If any sick, now in hospital at Warrenton Junction, are not provided for, and able to be transported, he will have them loaded into the wagon train of his own corps (even should this necessitate the destruction of much baggage and regimental property), and carried to Manassas Junction. The very important duty devolved upon Major-Gen. Banks, the Major-General commanding the army of Virginia feels assured that he will discharge with intelligence, courage and fidelity.

The General Headquarters will be with the corps of Gen. Heintzelman until further notice.

By command of Major-Gen. Pope.

Geo. D. Ruggles, Colonel and Chief of Staff.

A true copy: T. C. H. Smith, Lieut.-Col. and A. D. C.

HEADQUARTERS ARMY OF VIRGINIA, ⎰
Aug. 27, 1862, 6:30 p. m., Bristow Station. ⎱

Maj.-Gen. F. J. Porter, Warrenton Junction.—General:—The Major-General commanding directs that you start at 1 o'clock to-night, and come forward with your whole Corps, or such part of it as is with you, so as to be here by daylight to-morrow morning. Hooker has had a very severe action with the enemy with a loss of about three hundred killed and wounded. The enemy has been driven back but is retiring along the railroad. We must drive him from Manassas and clear the country between that place and Gainesville, where McDowell is. If Morrill has not joined you, send him word to push forward immediately; also, send word to Banks to hurry forward with all speed to take your place at Warrenton Junction. It is necessary on all accounts that you should be here by daylight. I send an officer with this dispatch who will conduct you to this place. Be sure to send word to Banks, who is on the road from Fayetteville, probably in the direction of Bealton. Say to Banks, also, that he had best run back the railroad train to this side of Cedar Run. If he is not with you write him to that effect.

By command of Gen. Pope,

Geo, D. Ruggles, Col. and Chief of Staff.

P. S.—If Banks is not at Warrenton Junction, leave a regiment of infantry and two pieces of artillery as a guard till he comes up, with instructions to follow you immediately upon his doing so.

If Banks is not at the Junction instruct Col. Clary to run the trains back to this side of Cedar Run, and post a regiment and a section of artillery with it.

By command of Gen. Pope.

Geo D. Ruggles, Col. and Chief of Staff.

A true copy: T. C. H. Smith, Lieut.-Col. and A. D. C.

HEADQUARTERS, BRISTOW, Aug. 27, 1862—9 p. m.

Major-General Kearney:—At the very earliest blush of dawn push forward with your command with all speed to this place. You cannot be more than three or four miles distant. Jackson, A. P. Hill and Ewell are in front of us. Hooker has had a severe fight with them to-day. McDowell marches upon Manassas Junction from Gainesville to-morrow at daybreak. Reno upon the same place at the same hour. I want you here at day-dawn, if possible, and we shall bag the whole crowd. Be prompt and expeditious, and never mind wagon trains or roads till this affair is over. Lieut. Brooks will deliver you this communication. He has one for Gen.:Reno and one for Gen. McDowell. Please have these dispatches sent forward instantly by a trusty staff officer, who will be sure to deliver them without fail, and make him bring back a receipt to you before daylight. Lieut. Brooks will remain with you and bring you to this camp. Use the cavalry I send you to escort your staff officer to McDowell and Reno.

John Pope, Major-General Commanding.

A true copy: T. C. H. Smith, Lieut.-Col. and A. D. C.

HEADQUARTERS, ARMY OF VIRGINIA, {
Bristow Station, Aug. 22d, 1862—9 o'clock p. m. {

Major-General McDowell:—At daylight to-morrow morning march rapidly on Manassas Junction with your whole force, resting your right on the Manassas Gap Railroad, throwing your left well to the east. Jackson, Ewell and A. P. Hill are between Gainesville and Manasass Junction. We had a severe fight with them to-day, driving them back several miles along the railroad. If you will march promptly and rapidly at the earliest dawn of day upon Manassas Junction, we shall bag the whole crowd. I have directed Reno to march from Greenwich at the same hour upon Manassas Junction, and Kearney, who is in his rear, to march on Bristow at daybreak. Be expeditious and the day is our own.

John Pope, Major-General Commanding.

A true copy: T. C. H. Smith, Lieut.-Col. and A. D. C.

HEADQUARTERS ARMY OF VIRGINIA, {
Bristow Station, Aug. 28, 1862—10:40 a. m. {

Maj.-Gen. Banks, Warrenton Junction—General:—Maj.-General Pope directs me to say that as soon as the railroad trains and all public property shall have been safely run back from Warrenton Junction you will move your command back to Kettle Run Bridge, where you will find the railroad obstructed and the railroad trains stopped.

You will there take the same measures to save the public property from attack by the enemy as directed in copy of General Orders from these headquarters, sent to you yesterday through Maj.-Gen. Porter.

I am, General, very respectfully, your ob't serv't,

(Signed.)   Geo. D. Ruggles, Col. and Chief of Staff.

A true copy: T. C. H. Smith, Lt.-Col. and A. D. C.

HEADQUARTERS ARMY OF VIRGINIA, }
Bristow Station, Aug. 28, 1862—10:50 a. m. }

Col. Clary, Chief Quartermaster Army of Virginia :—Maj.-Gen. Pope directs that all the wagon trains be kept closed up and close in rear of the troops. You will accordingly give instructions to the various subordinate Quartermasters, including Regimental Quartermasters, to keep their trains closed and immediately in rear of the troops. Please see that this order is executed.

By command of Maj.-Gen. Pope.
(Signed.)   Geo. D. Ruggles, Col. and Chief of Staff.
A true copy : T. C. H. Smith, Lieut.-Col. and A. D. C.

HEADQUARTERS, Army of VIRGINIA, }
Bristow Station, Aug. 28, 1862—11 a. m. }

Surgeon McParlin, Medical Director Army of Virginia—Sir :—Maj.-Gen. Pope directs that you take measures to hunt up the wounded of the enemy, and to provide for them the same as for our own soldiers.   I am, Sir, very respectfully, your ob't serv't,
(Signed.)   Geo. D. Ruggles, Col. and Chief of Staff.
A true copy : T. C. H. Smith, Lieut.-Col. and A. D. C.

HEADQUARTERS ARMY OF VIRGINIA, }
Bristow Station, Aug. 28, 1862—11:10 a. m. }

Lieut. F. J. Shunk, Chief of Ordnance, Army of Virginia :—The Major-General Commanding directs that one or two boxes of ammunition be thrown into every wagon that passes the railroad train where the ammunition now is, no matter to whom the wagon or wagon train belongs.

By Command of Maj.-Gen. Pope.
(Signed.)   Geo. D. Ruggles, Col. and Chief of Staff.
A true copy : T. C. H. Smith, Lieut.-Col. and A. D. C.

HEADQUARTERS, ARMY OF VIRGINIA, }
Aug. 28, 1862. }

Special Order No. —.—The trains will come forward in the following order, viz :

1st. Heintzelman's.   3d. Sigel's.
2d. McDowell's.   4th. Porter's.

All the supply and regimental trains will be sent forward to this place as rapidly as possible—ammunition being forwarded in advance of all other supplies.

By command of Maj.-Gen. Pope.
(Signed.)   Geo. D. Ruggles, Col. and Chief of Staff.
A true copy : T. C. H. Smith, Lieut.-Col., and A. D. C.

HEADQUARTERS ARMY OF VIRGINIA, }
Bristow Station, Aug. 28, 1862—11:20 a. m. }

Col. Clary, Chief Quartermaster Army of Virginia :—The Major-General commanding directs that one or two boxes of ammunition be thrown into every wagon that passes the railroad train where the ammunition now is, no matter to whom the wagon or wagon train belongs. He also directs that the railroad trains be unloaded into the passing wagon trains in the same manner, commencing first to unload the ammunition as hereinbefore directed.

By command of Major-Gen. Pope.
(Signed.)   Geo. D. Ruggles, Col. and Chief of Staff.
A true copy: T. C. H. Smith, Lieut.-Col. and A. D. C.

HEADQUARTERS ARMY OF VIRGINIA, }
Manassas Junction, Aug. 28, 1862—1:20 p. m. }

Maj.-General McDowell:—I sent you a dispatch a few minutes ago directing you to move on Gum Springs to intercept Jackson. Since then I have received your note of this morning. I will this evening push forward Reno to Gainesville, and follow with Heintzelman, unless there is a large force of the enemy at Centreville, which I do not believe. Ascertain if you can about this. I do not wish you to carry out the order to proceed to Gum Spring if you consider it too hazardous, but I will support you in any way you suggest, by pushing forward from Manassas Junction across the turnpike. Jackson has a large train which should certainly be captured. Give me your views fully. You know the country much better than I do. Come no further in this direction with your command but call back what has advanced thus far.

John Pope, Maj.-Gen. Commanding.
A true copy : T. C. H. Smith, Lt.-Col. and A. D. C.

HEADQUARTERS, ARMY OF VIRGINIA, NEAR BULL RUN, }
Aug. 28, 1862—9:50 p. m. }

Major-Gen. Kearney—General:—Gen. McDowell has intercepted the retreat of the enemy and is now in his front, Sigel on the right of McDowell. Unless he can escape by by-paths leading to the north to-night he must be captured. I desire you to move forward at 1 o'clock to-night, even if you can carry with you no more than 2000 men, though I trust you will carry the larger part of your division. Pursue the turnpike from Centreville to Warrenton. The enemy is not more than three and a half miles from you. Seize any of the people of the town to guide you. Advance cautiously and drive in the enemy's pickets to-night, and at early dawn attack him vigorously. Hooker shall be close behind you. Extend your right well toward the north and push forward your right wing well in the attack. Be sure to march not later than one, with all the men you can take.

John Pope, Major-General Commanding.
A true copy: T. C. H. Smith, Lieut.-Col. and A. D. C.

HEADQUARTERS ARMY OF VIRGINIA, NEAR BULL RUN, }
Aug. 28, 1862—10 p. m. }

Major-General Heintzelman,—General: Gen. McDowell has intercepted the retreat of the enemy. Sigel is immediately on his right, and I see no possibility of his escape. I have instructed Kearney to push forward cautiously at 1 o'clock to-night until he drives in the pickets of the enemy and to assault him vigorously at daylight in the morning. It is of the last importance that Hooker should be close in his rear. I desire, therefore, that Hooker shall march at 3 o'clock to night, taking the turnpike from Centreville to Warrenton, and resting on that road 1½ miles beyond Centreville, as reserve for Kearney.—Send a copy of this dispatch to Hooker immediately, and I beg you particularly to see that Hooker marches at the hour specified, even if he should have to do so with one-half of his men. I shall rely upon this. John Pope, Major-General Commanding.

A true copy: T. C. H. Smith, Lt.-Col. and A. D. C.

Dispatches and Orders sent and received from Aug. 29, to Sept. 2 Inclusive.

HEADQUARTERS, ARMY OF VIRGINIA, NEAR BULL RUN }
Aug. 29, 1862—3 a. m. }

Maj.-Gen. Porter—General:—McDowell has intercepted the retreat of Jackson. Sigel is immediately on the right of McDowell.—Kearney and Hooker march to attack the enemy's rear at early dawn. Major-Gen. Pope directs you to move upon Centreville at the first dawn of day with your whole command, leaving your trains to follow. It is very important that you should be here at a very early hour in the morning. A severe engagement is likely to take place, and your presence is necessary.

I am, General, very respectfully, your ob't serv't.

Geo D. Ruggles, Col. and Chief of Staff.

A true copy: T. C. H. Smith, Lt.-Col. and A. D. C.

HEADQUARTERS ARMY OF VIRGINIA, NEAR BULL RUN, }
August 29, 1862—5 a. m. }

Maj.-Gen. Reno—General:—I sent you some verbal orders by Col. Smith last night. News from the front received since makes it necessary to modify them. You will accordingly move rapidly on Centreville by the road past these headquarters. Upon arriving at Centreville you will take the turnpike toward Warrenton, and push forward rapidly. You will find the whole corps of Heintzelman in front of you. Pass his stragglers and keep well up with his command—pushing rapidly toward any heavy firing you may hear.

Jno. Pope, Maj.-Gen., Commanding.

A true copy: T. C. H. Smith, Lieut.-Col. and A. D. C.

HEADQUARTERS, ARMY OF VIRGINIA, }
Centreville, Aug. 30, 1862. }

General Order No. 5.—Gens. McDowell and Porter:—You will please move forward with your joint commands toward Gainesville. I sent Gen. Porter written orders to that effect an hour and a half ago. Heintzelman, Sigel and Reno are moving on the Warrenton turnpike, and must now be not far from Gainesville. I desire that, as soon as communication is established between this force and your own, the whole command shall halt. It may be necessary to fall back behind Bull Run, at Centreville to-night. I presume it will be so, on account of our supplies. I have sent no orders of any description to Ricketts, and none to interfere in any way with the movements of McDowell's troops, except what I sent by his Aid-de-Camp last night, which were to hold his position on the Warrenton pike, until the troops from here should fall upon the enemy's flank and rear. I do not even know Ricketts' position, as I have not been able to find out where Gen. Mc-Dowell was until a late hour this morning. Gen. McDowell will take immediate steps to communicate with Gen. Ricketts, and instruct him to rejoin the other divisions of his corps as soon as practicable. If any considerable advantages are to be gained by departing from this order, it will not be strictly carried out. One thing must be had in view, that the troops must occupy a position from which they can reach Bull Run to-night or by morning. The indications are that the whole force of the enemy is moving in this direction at a pace that will bring them here by to-morrow night or next day. My own headquarters will be for the present with Heintzelman's Corps, or at this place.

(Signed)   John Pope, Major-General Commanding.
A true copy: T. C. H. Smith, Lieut.-Col. and A. D. C.

HEADQUARTERS IN THE FIELD,
Aug. 29,—4·30 p. m.

Major General Porter :—Your line of march brings you in on the enemy's right flank. I desire you to push forward into action at once on the enemy's flank, and if possible on his rear, keeping your right in communication with Gen. Reynolds. The enemy is massed in the woods in front of us, but can be shelled out as soon as you engage their flank. Keep heavy reserves and use your batteries, keeping well closed to your right all the time. In case you are obliged to fall back, do so to your right and rear so as to keep you in close communication with the right wing.

John Pope, Major-General Commanding.
A true copy: T. C. H. Smith, Lieut-Col. A. D. C.

HEADQUARTERS ARMY OF VIRGINIA,
In the field, Aug. 29th, 1862—5 p. m.

Major General Banks—General :—I would prefer that you send your trains direct to Manassas Junction and Centreville. The road is clear, and there is no difficulty about it. Send them through as soon as you can. Send back working parties to try and get the railroad in sufficiently good order, that the trains may be worked back to Bull Run. This is of the last importance, and you cannot get it done too soon. Work night and day at it.

(Signed)   John Pope, Major-General Com'ding.
A true copy: T. C. H. Smith, Lieut.-Col. and A. D. C.

HEADQUARTERS, ARMY OF VIRGINIA, ⎰
In the field near Bull Run, Aug. 29, 1862—8-50 p. m. ⎱

Major-General F. J. Porter—General:—Immediately upon the receipt of this order, the precise hour of receiving which you will acknowledge, you will march your command to the field of battle of to-day, and report to me in person for orders. You are to understand that you are expected to comply strictly with this order, and to be present on the field within three hours after its receipt, or after daybreak to-morrow morning.

John Pope, Major-General Commanding.

A true copy: T. C. H. Smith, Lieut.-Col. and A. D. C.

To Commanding Officer at Centreville:—I have been instructed by Gen. McClellan to inform you that he will have all the available wagons at Alexandria loaded with rations for your troops, and all of the cars, also, as soon as you will send in a cavalry escort to Alexandria as a guard to the train,

August 29, 1862—8 p. m.

Respectfully, W. B. Franklin, Maj.-Gen. Com'dg 6th Corps.

A true copy: T. C. H. Smith, Lieut.-Col. and A. D. C.

BULL RUN, ⎰
Aug. 30th, 1862—6-30 a. m. ⎱

Col. Clary, Chief Quartermaster, Army of Va.—Colonel:—You will immediately send to Alexandria an officer to bring out all supplies of forage and stores—forage particularly—required for this command. The stores will be brought to Fairfax by rail, and thence by wagon to Centreville. The officers sent by you will obtain from the commanding officer at Alexandria the escort necessary to protect the trains.

By command of Gen. Pope.

Geo. D. Ruggles, Col. and Chief of Staff.

A true copy: T. C. H. Smith, Lieut.-Col. and A. D. C.

HEADQUARTERS ARMY OF VIRGINIA, ⎰
Battle-field near Groveton, Aug. 30th, 1862—9 a. m. ⎱

Col. Clary, Chief Quartermaster Army of Virginia: — Maj. Gen. Pope directs that you send two hundred and fifty (250) wagons to Major-General Banks, in order that he may remove his sick, and public property from his present position to Centreville or vicinity. I am, Colonel, very respectfully, your obedient servant,

(Signed) Geo. D. Ruggles, Col. and Chief of Staff.

A true copy: T. C. H. Smith, Lieut.-Col. and A. D. C.

HEADQUARTERS ARMY OF VIRGINIA, ⎰
Near Groveton, Aug. 30th. ⎱

Col. Beckwith, Chief Commissary Colonel:—Gen. Pope directs that all the wagons at Centreville be unloaded there, and the property stored. The wagons will then be sent to Sangster's Station to haul subsistence stores from that place to Centreville.

By command of Maj.-Gen. Pope.

[Signed] Geo. D. Ruggles, Col. and Chief of Staff.

A true copy: T. C. H. Smith, Lt.-Col. and A. D. C.

HEADQUARTERS, ARMY OF VIRGINIA, }
Aug. 30th, 1862—6 p. m. }

Gen. Franklin:—Post your command, and whatever other troops you can collect, and put them in the fortifications at, and other strong positions around, Centreville, and hold those positions to the last extremity.

By command of Gen. Pope.

Geo. D. Ruggles, Col. and Chief of Staff.

A true copy : T. C. H. Smith, Lieut.-Col. and A. D. C.

August 30th—6-45 p. m.

Col. Clary:—You will immediately put all the wagons, and everything that interferes with the range of artillery from the works at Centreville, a good distance to the rear, on the other side of the town —out of range of artillery from the works.

By command of Maj.-Gen. Pope.

(Signed) Geo. D. Ruggles, Col. and Chief of Staff.

A true copy : T. C. H. Smith, Lieut.-Col. and A. D. C.

August 30th, 1862—3 p. m.

Gen. Heintzelman—[To be opened and read by Gens. Kearney and Hooker,]—*General :*—Retire to Centreville to-night with your command. If possible go by the 'way of Sudley's Ford. Gen. Reno commands the rear guard on the turnpike by which the balance of the army will fall back. Upon your arrival at Centreville, you will assemble your command on the north side of that town. Early in the morning proper positions will be assigned you.

By command of Major-Gen. Pope.

(Signed) Geo. D. Ruggles, Col. and Chief of Staff.

A true copy : T. C. H. Smith, Lt.-Col. and A. D. C.

HEADQUARTERS ARMY OF VIRGINIA, }
Centreville, Aug. 30, 1862. }

Special Orders No.—.The prisoners of war now at this place will be sent to morrow to Washington City, under guard of one regiment of infantry, to be furnished for this purpose by Major-Gen. McDowell.

By command of Major-General Pope,

(Signed) Geo D. Ruggles, Col. and Chief of Staff.

A true copy ; T. C. H. Smith, Lieut.-Col. and A. D. C.

CENTREVILLE, Aug. 30, 1862—9:45 p. m.

Maj.-Gen. Halleck,—General in Chief:—We have had a terrific battle again to-day. The enemy, largely re-enforced, assaulted our

9

position early to-day. We held our ground firmly until 6 o'clock p. m., when the enemy, massing very heavy forces on our left, forced back that wing about half a mile. At dark we held that position. Under all the circumstances—both horses and men having been two days without food, and the enemy greatly outnumbering us—I thought it best to move back to this place at dark. The movement has been made in perfect order and without loss. The troops are in good heart and marched off the field without the least hurry or confusion. Their conduct was very fine. The battle was most furious for hours, without cessation, and the losses on both sides very heavy. The enemy is badly whipped, and we shall do well enough. Do not be uneasy.— We will hold our own here. The labors and hardships of this army for two or three weeks have been beyond description. We have delayed the enemy as long as possible without losing the army. We have damaged him heavily, and I think the army entitled to the gratitude of the country. Be easy; everything will go well.

[Signed]   Jno. Pope, Major-General.

P. S.—We have lost nothing—neither guns nor wagons.

August 30, 1862—6:30 p. m.

Gen. Banks :—Destroy the public property at Bristow, and fall back upon Centreville at once. Destroy all the railroad property. Your troops at Bristow will withdraw through Brentsville. Your troops at Manassas and between there and Bristow will withdraw to Centreville.

By command of Major-Gen. Pope.

(Signed,)   Geo D. Ruggles, Col. and Chief of Staff.

A true copy: T. C. H. Smith, Lt.-Col. and A. D. C.

WASHINTON, Aug. 31st, 1862—11 a. m.

Major-Gen. Pope,—My dear General :—You have done nobly.— Don't yield another inch if you can avoid it. All reserves are being sent forward. Couch's Division goes to-day, part of it went to Sangster's Station last night with Franklin and Sumner, who must be now with you. Can't you renew the attack? I don't write more particularly for fear the dispatch will not reach you. I am doing all in my power for you and your noble army. God bless you and it. Send me news more often if possible.

(Signed,)   H. W. Halleck, Gen.-in-Chief

A true copy: T. C. H. Smith, Lieut.-Col. and A. D. C.

HEADQUARTERS ARMY OF VIRGINIA. }
Camp near Centreville, Aug. 31, 1862. }

(Circular.)

Commanders of Army Corps will forthwith establish suitable grand guards in front of the positions they respectively hold, and have outposts thrown forward which shall furnish a line of sentinels covering the entire army. Those on the flanks will furnish a grand guard for the flanks. The advanced position this side of Cub Run will only be held as an outpost, and the division now there will be withdrawn.

By command of Major-Gen. Pope.

(Signed,)   Geo D. Ruggles, Col. and Chief of Staff.

A true copy : T. C. H. Smith, Lieut. Col. and A. D. C.

(Circular to Corps Commanders.)

HEADQUARTERS ARMY OF VIRGINIA, }
Centreville, Aug. 31, 1862—8:30 a. m. }

General:—The Major-General commanding the Army of Virginia directs me to instruct you to take measures immediately to bring forward and distribute ammunition for your command.

1. Men should be selected to guide the wagons to the troops to be supplied, to report to Lieut.-Col. Smith, A. D. C., at these Headquarters.

2. A report of the amount and kind of ammunition required in your command should be made to Lieut.-Col Smith.

3. Empty wagons should be collected and sent to report to Lieut.. Col. Smith.

With great respect General, your obedient servant,

[Signed]   T. C. H. Smith, Lieut.-Col. and A. D. C.

A true copy : E. Haight, Capt. and A. D. C.

HEADQUARTERS ARMY OF VIRGINIA, }
Centreville, Aug. 31, 1862. }

[Circular,]

Commanding officers of Army Corps will send back to Alexandria all wagons appertaining to their trains, except those absolutely necessary to haul subsistence stores and ammunition from Fairfax Court-House to this place for their respective Corps. This movement will be under charge of Col. Clary, Chief Quartermaster, Army of Virginia.

By command of Major-Gen. Pope.

[Signed,]   Geo. D. Ruggles, Col. and Chief of Staff.

A true copy : T. C. H. Smith, Lieut.-Col. and A. D. C.

HEADQUARTERS ARMY OF VIRGINIA, }
Centreville, Aug. 31st, 1862—10:45 o'clock a. m. }

Maj.-General Halleck, General-in-Chief:—Our troops are all here, and in position, though much used up and worn out. I think perhaps it would have been greatly better if Sumner and Franklin had been here three or four days ago; but you may rely upon our giving them as desperate a fight as I can force our men to stand up to.

I should like to know whether you feel secure about Washington, should this army be destroyed. I shall fight it as long as a man will stand up to the work. You must judge what is to be done, having in view the safety of the Capital.

The enemy is already pushing a cavalry reconnoissance in front of Cub Run, whether in advance of an attack to-day, I do not yet know. I send you this that you may know our position and my purpose.

(Signed)   John Pope, Major-General Commanding.

A true copy : T. C. H. Smith, Lieut.-Col. and A. D. C.

HEADQUARTERS ARMY OF VIRGINIA, }
Centreville, Aug. 31st, 1862. }

Special Orders No—.—Carrol's Brigade of Ricketts' Division will proceed at once to Fairfax Station, and take post as a guard for commissary stores at that point. The commanding officer of these troops will report upon his arrival at Fairfax Station to Col. E. G. Beckwith, Chief Commissary Army of Virginia.

By command of Major-Gen. Pope.
(Signed) Geo. D. Ruggles, Col. and Chief of Staff.
A true copy: T. C. H. Smith, Lt.-Col. and A. D. C.

HEADQUARTERS ARMY OF VIRGINIA, }
Centreville, August, 31st, 1862. }

Commanding Officer Forces at Fairfax Court House,—Sir :— Maj.-Gen. Pope directs you at once to send two regiments of infantry and two pieces of artillery, to escort the wagon train now en route to Alexandria, as far as Cloud's Mills.

I am, Sir, very respectfully your obedient servant,
(Signed) Geo. D. Ruggles, Col. and Chief of Staff.
A true copy: T. C. H. Smith, Lt.-Col. and A. D. C.

Centreville, Aug. 31st.

Dear General :—Your dispatch of 11 a. m. has been received, and I thank you for your considerate commendation. I would be glad to have it in such shape that the army might be acquainted with it. We shall fight to the last. The whole Secession Army engaged us yesterday. I had a letter from Lee this morning. Ewell is killed ; Jackson badly wounded ; other generals of less note wounded. The plan of the enemy will undoubtedly be to turn my flank. If he does so, he will have his hands full. My troops are in good heart. I need cavalry horses terribly. Send me ten thousand, in lots, and under strong escort. I have never yet received a single one.

(Signed) John Pope, Major-General.
A true copy: T. C. H. Smith, Lieut.-Col., and A. D. C.

HEADQUARTERS ARMY OF VIRGINIA, }
Camp near Centreville, Sept. 1, 1862—3 a. m. }

Maj.-Gen. Sumner :—The reconnoitering party of cavalry which you sent out yesterday morning, under Capt. Haight, has, as I am informed, been captured by the enemy's cavalry. It is essential that your right be carefully watched. I desire you at daylight to push a reconnoissance of not less than one brigade, supported if necessary by a second, toward the north of your position, to the Little River turnpike, and beyond. The direction of your reconnoissance should be as nearly due north as practicable, and should be pushed not less than five miles. It is of great importance that this reconnoissance should be made at an early hour in the morning. The orderly whom you sent to me left me without any permission, so that I find it very difficult to find your headquarters. Please send him back.

(Signed) John Pope, Maj.-Gen. Commanding.

A true copy : T. C. H. Smith, Lieut.-Col. and A. D. C.

HEADQUARTERS ARMY OF VIRGINIA, }
Centreville, Sept. 1st, 1862. }

General :—The Major-General Commanding directs me to inform you that a large supply of ammunition has arrived since yesterday, say 120 wagons, and that near the earthwork, close in rear of Centreville, an officer will be found, charged with its distribution. The ammunition will be kept in the wagons in which it came, so as to be sent forward to the troops to be supplied immediately when required.

Major-General Commanding, &c.,

With great respect, General, your ob'dt serv't,

(Signed) T. C. H. Smith, Lieut.-Col. and A. D. C.

A true copy : T. C. H. Smith, Lieut.-Col. and A. D. C.

HEADQUARTERS ARMY OF VIRGINIA, }
September 1st—5·45 a. m. }

Major-General E. V. Sumner,—General:—The reconnoissance is only designed to ascertain whether there is any considerable movement of the enemy's infantry towards our right and rear. We have no cavalry—not a horse that can possibly perform service, and it may be necessary, in order to obtain the information I desire, to drive off the enemy's cavalry. I do not care that the brigade shall be pushed further than the Little River Turnpike, while skirmishers are thrown still further, in order fully to ascertain whether the enemy is making any movement toward Germantown and Fairfax Court-House. I do not wish any engagement brought on at present on that ground, but when the information required shall have been obtained by the brigade, withdraw it.

[Signed] Jno. Pope, Maj.-Gen. Commanding.

A true copy : T. C. H. Smith, Lieut.-Col. and A. D. C.

HEADQUARTERS OF THE ARMY, }
Washington, D. C., Sept. 1, 1862. }

Gen. Pope :—Yours of last evening was received at 4 a. m. this morning. I want to issue a complimentary order, but as you are daily fighting, it could hardly be distributed. I will do so very soon.

Look out well for your right, and don't let the enemy get between you and the forts. We are strengthening the line of defence as rapidly as possible. Horses will be sent to you to-day. Send dispatches to me as often as possible. I hope for an arrival of cavalry to-day.

Yours truly, H. W. Halleck, Gen.-in-Chief.

P. S.—Acknowledge hour of receipt of this.

A true copy : T. C. H. Smith, Lieut.-Col. and A. D. C.

CENTREVILLE, Sept. 1—8:50 a. m.

Major-Gen. Halleck, General-in-Chief:—All was quiet yesterday and so far this morning. My men all resting. They need it much. Forage for our horses is being brought up. Our cavalry is completely broken down, so that there are not five horses to a company that can raise a trot. The consequence is that I am forced to keep considerable infantry along the roads in my rear to make them secure, and even then it is difficult to keep the enemy's cavalry off the roads. I shall attack again to-morrow if I can, the next day certainly.

I think it my duty to call your attention to the unsoldierly and dangerous conduct of many brigade, and some division commanders of the forces sent here from the Peninsula. Every word and act and intention is discouraging, and calculated to break down the spirits of the men and to produce disaster. One commander of a corps who was ordered to march from Manassas Junction to join me near Groveton, although he was only five miles distant, failed to get up at all, and worse still, fell back to Manassas without a fight, and in plain hearing, at less than three miles distance, of a furious battle, which raged all day. It was only in consequence of peremptory orders that he joined me next day. One of his brigades, the Brigadier-General of which professed to be looking for his Division, absolutely remained all day at Centreville, in plain view of the battle, and made no attempt to join. What renders the whole matter worse, these are both officers of the regular army, who do not hold back from ignorance or fear. Their constant talk, indulged in publicly and in promiscuous company, is that "the Army of the Potomac will not fight," that they are demoralized by withdrawal from the Peninsula, &c. When such example is set by officers of high rank, the influence is very bad among those in subordinate stations.

You have hardly an idea of the demoralization among officers of high rank in the Potomac Army, arising in all instances from personal feeling in relation to changes of Commander-in-Chief and others. These men are mere tools or parasites, but their example is producing, and must necessarily produce, very disastrous results. You should know these things, as you alone can stop it. Its source is beyond my reach, though its effects are very perceptible and very dangerous. I am endeavoring to do all I can, and will most assuredly put them where they shall fight or run away. My advice to you (I give it with freedom, as I know you will not misunderstand it), is, that in view of any satisfactory results, you draw back this army to the intrenchments in front of Washington, and set to work in that secure place to reorganize and rearrange it. You may avoid great disaster by doing so. I do not consider the matter except in a purely military light, and it is bad enough and great enough to make some action very necessary. Where there is no heart in their leaders, and every disposition to hang back, much cannot be expected from the men.

Please hurry forward cavalry horses to me under strong escort. I need them badly, worse than I can tell you.

[Signed]   John. Pope, Major-General.

A true copy: T. C. H. Smith, Lieut.-Col. and A. D. C.

HEADQUARTERS ARMY OF VIRGINIA, }
Near Centreville, Sept. 1. 1862. }

Maj.-Gen. Franklin,— General :—Gen. Pope directs you to establish your grand guards on the pike from Centreville to Warrenton.—An outpost of one regiment of infantry and two pieces of artillery of Reynolds' division has been ordered to take post on the same road.

I am, General, very respectfully, your ob't serv't.

[Signed,] Geo D. Ruggles, Col. and Chief of Staff.
A true copy: T. C. H. Smith, Lieut.-Col. and A. D. C.

HEADQUARTERS ARMY OF VIRGINIA, }
Near Centreville, Sept. 1, 1862. }

To the Officer Commanding the forces around Fairfax Court-House :
—Gen. Pope directs that you furnish one regiment of infantry as an escort for a wagon train from Fairfax Court-House to Fairfax Station. Lieut. Devens, 9th Infantry, will call for the escort as he proceeds through the town.

I am, Sir, very respectfully your obedient servant,

(Signed,) Geo D. Ruggles, Col. and Chief of Staff.
A true copy: T. C. H. Smith, Lt. Col. and A. D. C.

HEADQUARTERS ARMY OF VIRGINIA, }
Centreville, Sept. 1, 1862—11 oclock, a. m. }

Maj.-Gen. Halleck :—The enemy is deploying his forces on the Little River Pike, and preparing to advance by that road on Fairfax Court-House. This movement turns Centreville, and interposes between us and Washington, and will force me to attack his advance, which I shall do as soon as his movement is sufficiently developed. I have nothing like the force you undoubtedly suppose, and the fight will be necessarilly desperate. I hope you will make all preparations to make a vigorous defence of the intrenchments around Washington.

[Signed,] John Pope, Maj.-Gen. Commanding.
A true copy : T. C. H. Smith, Lieut.-Col. and A. D. C.

CENTREVILLE, Sept. 1, 1862,—12 m.

Maj.-Gen. McDowell :—You will march rapidly back to Fairfax C. H. with your whole division, assuming command of the two brigades now there, and immediately occupy Germantown with your whole force, so as to cover the turnpike from this place to Alexandria. Jackson is reported advancing on Fairfax with twenty thousand men. Move quickly.

(Signed,) John Pope, Major-Gen. Commanding.
A true copy: T. C. H. Smith, Lieut.-Col. and A. D. C.

HEADQUARTERS, ARMY OF VIRGINIA, }
Centreville, Sept. 1, 1862—1 p. m. }

Major-Gen. Hooker :—You will at once proceed to Germantown, assume command of the troops arriving at Fairfax Court-House, together with the brigades now under command of Cols. Torbert and Hincks.

By command of Major-Gen. Pope.

(Signed,)   Geo E. Ruggles, Col. and Chief of Staff.

A true copy: T. C. H. Smith, Lieut. Col. and A. D. C.

HEADQUARTERS ARMY OF VIRGINIA, }
Centreville, Sept. 1, 1862—12:30 p. m. }

Col. A. T. Torbert, Comd'g Brigade near Fairfax C. H.—Move your brigade at once to Germantown, and join it to the one under Col. Hincks at that place. Maj.-Gen. Hooker is assigned to the command of the forces arriving at Fairfax C. H. from Washington, together with those stationed at Germantown.

By command of Maj.-Gen. Pope.

(Signed,)   Geo. D. Ruggles, Col. and Chief of Staff.

A true copy: T. C. H. Smith, Lieut. Col. and A. D. C.

NEAR CENTREVILLE, Sept. 1, 1862—4 p. m.

Maj. Gen. McDowell:—If you hear a battle raging to night near Centreville, advance to the north, keeping your communications open with Reno, and near to him; also, by the right with Hooker, who will advance his left to your right.

By command of Major-Gen. Pope.

(Signed,)   Geo D. Ruggles, Col. and Chief of Staff.

A true copy: T. C. H. Smith, Lieut. Col. and A. D. C.

HEADQUARTERS ARMY OF VIRGINIA, }
Fairfax C. H., Sept. 1, 1862. }

General Orders No.—: The Army Corps of Heintzelman, Sigel, Sumner, Porter and Reno, as soon after daylight as possible, will begin to draw slowly to their right in the direction of Fairfax Court-House, until they come closely in contact with each other. Major-Gen. Reno will follow as closely as possible the line of the old Railroad now occupied by him, the others along the pike. He will notify those in his rear of his exact position, and every step of his movements, and will ask support if he needs it. They will not be more than half a mile in rear of him. If any severe engagement should occur at any point of the line, the army corps commanders nearest on the right and left will immediately send forward a staff officer to report to the General commanding the troops of the attack, and to notify him that they stand ready to support him if he needs it. For the present, the general headquarters will be established at Fairfax Court-House.

By command of Major-Gen. Pope.

[Signed,]   Geo D. Ruggles, Col. and Chief of Staff.

A true copy: T. C. H. Smith, Lieut Col. and A. D. C.

HEADQUARTERS ARMY OF VIRGINIA, }
Centreville, Sept. 1st, 1862—2 p. m. }

Col. Torbert: — Send back word immediately to Alexandria to hurry up Couch's Division, and all the troops coming from Washington to Germantown. They must be at Germantown as early this afternoon as possible—certainly to night. They must take up strong positions there. There is no doubt the enemy is approaching you. Hold on to your position to the last. The whole army is on the move to join you.

By command of Major-General Pope.

.[Signed]   Geo. D. Ruggles, Col. and Chief of Staff.

A true copy : T. C. H. Smith, Lieut.-Col. and A. D. C.

———

FAIRFAX COURT HOUSE, Sept. 2d, 1862.

Major-General Halleck, Washington :—As I expected, the enemy last evening attacked my right furiously in the direction of Fairfax C. H., but were repulsed with heavy loss. Our loss was also severe. Gens. Stevens being killed, and Kearney missing. The enemy has not renewed the attack this morning, but is undoubtedly again beating around to the north-east. Your telegram of this date is just received, and its provisions will be carried out at once.

[Signed]   John Pope, Maj.-Gen. Commanding.

A true copy : T. C. H. Smith, Lieut.-Col. and A. D. C.

———

HEADQUARTERS ARMY OF VIRGINIA, }
Fairfax Court House, Sept. 2d, 1862.
[Circular.]

The following movements of troops will at once be made, in accordance with the instruction from the War Department, viz. :

1. Banks' Corps will march by the Braddock Road and Annandale, and take post at or near Fort North.

2. The Corps of Franklin and Hooker will pursue the Little River Pike toward Alexandria.

3. Heintzelman's Corps, the Braddock Road toward Fort Lyon.

McDowell's Corps, the road by Fall's Church, Little River and Columbia Pike toward Forts Craig and Tyllinghast. The Corps of Porter, Sumner and Sigel, via Vienna, toward the Chain Bridge. These three latter Corps will keep well closed up, and within easy supporting distance of each other.

The cavalry under Gen. Buford will follow and cover the march of the three Corps of Porter, Sumner and Sigel; and Bayard the troops marching on the road south of it. Sumner will bring up the rear on the route he is ordered to pursue. Hooker will cover the rear on the Little River Pike, and Banks the rear on the Braddock Road. Gen. Banks will call in the forces from Sangster's and Fairfax Stations, and will break up the depot at the latter place, shipping all stores by rail to Alexandria. The wagon trains, except such as are in immediate use by the Corps, will pursue the Little River Pike to Alexandria. The commanding officers of Corps will send forward a capable officer to Alexandria to take charge of their respective trains, and will conduct them to the headquarters of their respective Corps. The Medical Director will take immediate steps to have all the sick and wound-

10

ed carried back to Alexandria. Gen. Reno will take up the line of march immediately by the Little River Turnpike to Alexandria.— The commanders of these various Army Corps will send forward, several hours in advance, Staff Officers to notify Gen. McClellan of their approach to the points which they are to occupy.

By order of Major-Gen. Pope.

Geo D. Ruggles, Col. and Chief of Staff.

A true copy: T. C. H. Smith, Lieut.-Col and A. D. C.

HEADQUARTERS ARMY OF VIRGINIA, }
Fairfax, Sept. 2d, 1862, }

Maj.-Gen. Halleck:—The whole army is returning in good order, without confusion, or the slightest loss of property. The enemy has made no advances this morning, owing no doubt to his severe loss last evening. Three army corps pursue the route via Vienna to Chain Bridge, covered by all the effective cavalry. Ten corps by the Braddock road. These last corps are ordered to break up the depot at Fairfax Station, call in the troops from Sangster's and elsewhere on the railroad, and to move back to Alexandria. Our whole wagon train is far in advance of us toward the same place. Our whole force is less than 60,000 men. Everything is being safely moved back to the intrenchments. When the stragglers can be assembled, our force will be largely increased, I shall leave here with the last and encamp to-night near Ball's Cross Roads.

(Signed,) Jno. Pope, Maj.-Gen. Com.

A true copy: T. C. H. Smith, Lieut,-Col. and A. D. C.

NEW YORK, Jan. 27, 1863.

A dispatch was received from Maj.-Gen. Banks on the second of September stating that the wagon trains in his charge had all been brought in safely. Nothing lost. This dispatch has been mislaid.

T. C. H. Smith, Lt.-Col. and A. D. C.

HEADQUARTERS ARMY OF VIRGINIA, }
Ball's Cross Roads, Sept. 2, 1862—7:10 p. m. }

Major-Gen. Halleck,— General-in chief, Washington:—I arrived here safely. Command coming in on the road without much molestation. Some artillery firing on the roads through Vienna and Chain Bridge, but nothing of a serious character so far as I can learn.— Within an hour all the commands on the other roads will be in camp within the intrenchments. The three corps on the Vienna and Chain Bridge roads by to-morrow morning. I await your orders. The enemy still continue to beat around to the north. I do not myself believe that any attack here is contemplated. The troops are very weary, but otherwise in good condition.

(Signed,) John Pope, Major-Gen. Com'g.

A true copy: T. C. H. Smith, Lieut.-Col. and A. D. C.

www.ingramcontent.com/pod-product-compliance
Lightning Source LLC
Chambersburg PA
CBHW020231090426
42735CB00010B/1651